Disappearance: A Map

PREVIOUSLY PUBLISHED TITLES
BY SHEILA NICKERSON

POETRY

Feast of the Animals: An Alaska Bestiary, Volumes 1 and 2
In the Compass of Unrest
On Why the Quilt-Maker Became a Dragon
Waiting for the News of Death
Songs of the Pine-Wife
To the Waters and the Wild: Poems of Alaska
Letter from Alaska and Other Poems

FICTION

In Rooms of Falling Rain

NONFICTION

Writers in the Public Library

Disappearance: A Map

A Meditation on Death and Loss in the High Latitudes

SHEILA NICKERSON

A Harvest Book

Harcourt Brace & Company

San Diego   New York   London

Requests for permission to make copies of any part of the work should
be mailed to: Permissions Department, Harcourt Brace & Company,
6277 Sea Harbor Drive, Orlando, Florida 32887-6777.

This Harvest edition is published by arrangement with Doubleday,
a division of Bantam Doubleday Dell Publishing Group.

Library of Congress Cataloging-in-Publication Data
Nickerson, Sheila B.
Disappearance—a map: a meditation on death and loss
in the high latitudes/Sheila Nickerson.—1st Harvest ed.
p.   cm.—(A Harvest Book)
Includes bibliographical references.
ISBN 0-15-600498-4
1. Nickerson, Sheila B.—Homes and haunts—Alaska.
2. Wilderness areas—Alaska. 3. Missing persons—Alaska.
4. Loss (Psychology) 5. Death—Alaska. I. Title.
PS3564.I288Z47 1997
979.8'05—DC21   97-4446

Design by Marysarah Quinn
Printed in the United States of America
First Harvest edition 1997
A C E D B

Contents

Disappearances, apparitions; few clues, or none at all. Mostly it isn't murder, a punishable crime—the people just vanish. They go away, in sorrow, in pain, in mute astonishment, as of something decided forever. But sometimes you can't be sure, and a thing will happen that remains so unresolved, so strange, that someone will think of it years later; and he will sit there in the dusk and silence, staring out the window at another world.

— JOHN HAINES, "Lost,"
from *The Stars, the Snow, the Fire*

Disappearance: A Map

CHAPTER I

Lost

I live in a place where people disappear. Alaska. Too large to comprehend.

People go out in planes, boats, on foot, and are never heard from again.

It is May, almost spring but still a time of potentially cruel weather, especially in the tumultuous arc of the Gulf of Alaska, the place where the North American and Pacific plates meet and violence is upheaved in tectonic battle. It is a place of earthquake, young mountains, and volatile glaciers, a place where the pressure of frozen millennia breaks in blue ice against a stormy sea, a place where exquisitely sharp peaks throw back the weather that tries to move inland from that sea.

Somewhere in this unvisited place a colleague has disappeared. Kent Roth, a fishery biologist with the Alaska Department of Fish and Game, has gone down with two brothers and two friends on a flight from Yakutat to Anchorage. It is an immense area, one that has swallowed people from the earliest times of its recorded history.

Kent, his brothers Scott and Jeff, and their friends Brian Barber and Tim Thornton—all from Anchorage—had been fishing for steelhead, a species becoming ever rarer in Alaska, on the Situk River. They fished late, left late, in deteriorating weather. Their Cessna 340A took off from Yakutat at about 6 P.M. on Sunday, May 3. In the lengthening light of spring there should have been good visibility for the flight, but fog and icing conditions prevailed. A younger brother, Jason, had left Yakutat for Anchorage earlier in his own plane, in marginal weather. He was worried about his brothers. Except for a regular radio message from the plane a few minutes into the flight, as it reached an altitude of 12,000 feet, nothing was heard.

We can only conclude that ice forced it down into the vastness of ice, into itself. The area includes the Malaspina Glacier and the Bering Glacier, the two largest glaciers in North America—a torturous wilderness of snow and crevasse that has claimed many lives and left numerous mysteries. This immense area is sometimes referred to as Alaska's Bermuda Triangle.

At the office in Juneau, the state capital, we receive

5

information about how to donate annual leave to Kent. As long as he has leave, he will be given a paycheck. If he is declared dead, that leave will be translated into funds for his family.

The family keeps the search going. Their loyalty surges from the newspaper accounts, leaps with desperate energy off the page. I look at the telephone, which used to bring me Kent's voice, and at a recent memo from him. I talk to people in the office. Some, on their own time and at their own expense, are involved in the search.

I watch the papers unfold the story of the disappearance, as the story itself gradually slips off the front pages, moves into the back pages, then disappears from print. How many times before has this story been told? I ask myself. And what of the others who have disappeared, whose stories have dropped out of the newspapers and off the radio reports, or whose stories never were included because they happened before the era of mass media or because no one knew of them? Or cared? What of those not important enough to be searched for beyond the cursory attempt? What is it to disappear?

I remember how, almost twenty years ago, Alaska's only congressman, Nick Begich, and House Democratic leader Hale Boggs of Louisiana disappeared in the same area. And I know in the intervening twenty years there has been a long list of others. Usually the plane is never found. The area is too large, the crevasses and the snow too deep, the waters too quick and too cold. Often the search is over quickly, the names of the disappeared forgotten or never known.

At sea, boats go down, and those who fish are swept overboard. Seldom are the bodies found. Crabbing in the Bering Sea is the nation's most dangerous occupation, but the waters of Alaska are unkind on every coast and in every fishery.

And in the Bering Sea and other northern waters, crab pots break away from their moorings and ghost-fish on the bottom of the sea. And the bottom of the sea holds many mysteries.

On board the Alaska ferry M/V *Malaspina*, I watched the wake as we pulled away from Seattle. I watched it until Seattle disappeared in the dusk and the distance. I had no idea what lay ahead. Martin was waiting for us; he had gone ahead six weeks before to take a job with the Alaska Department of Highways and to find us a home. Other than him, our future there was a blank. I had with me six-year-old Helen and three-year-old Tom, along with their gerbils and a carload of what seemed important to carry from the past—from Colorado, where we had lived for seven years. The purser asked me if I would be happy in Juneau. I laughed. I had no way of knowing what he meant.

CHAPTER II

I Set Out

It is so hard to see! I didn't really know Kent—he was someone I talked to on the telephone but had never met. He worked in Anchorage and I worked in Juneau. A distance of more than five hundred miles by air over trackless mountains and ice separated us—that same distance into which he had fallen and vanished, where so many had fallen and vanished. Still, I felt compelled to confront his disappearance.

Perhaps it was because I had just turned fifty—what May Sarton calls the "meridian of fifty"—and was about to take early retirement. I was surrounded by change and loss, my children having grown into their own lives, many friends having died. I was standing on the brink of disappearance. I had to know what was there, the terrain, and whether Kent could be called back, whether anyone—ever—could be called back.

To know where I was going, first I had to know where I was—who I was.

Some points of reference were clear. I was a wife and a mother of three grown children, a government worker with a number of titles, among them editor of *Alaska's Wildlife*, the state conservation magazine. I was a writer whose life had consisted largely in crafting a bridge—or was it a web?—of poems. There had been some small successes and just enough in the way of kind letters and remarks from readers to keep me going, to let me know that what I looked upon as my real work as a poet was a shared work, one that did make a difference. What kept me on track, or so I thought, was the transcendence of the poem—the vault through time and space that lifted me to a place of harmony and meaning. That transcendence was my guiding force. I lived on the brink of the leap, hoping others might follow, at least partway. That was the purpose of my work, my life. And sometimes in dreams I flew.

As a writer I mapped, or tried to fix on the page, what otherwise was evanescent and fluid. Confronted with emotional pain, I took to the blank page to find my way out of it: the blizzard of atoms in a physics still not fixed. If only I could be alone with the poem, I could climb to a vantage point and look down with some understanding over an otherwise inexplicable landscape.

All my adult life I had searched for spiritual truth. Raised a Roman Catholic, I now followed a path based on personal choice in levels of consciousness. I had discarded sin and guilt but still feared emotion and self-revelation. I took comfort in quantum mechanics but still needed to set my own coordinates in time and space and suffered a deep need for "home." I knew that the veil between this world and the next was thin, that I was indeed touching it. But I did not know how to say boldly, It doesn't exist. Follow me, I'll show you. I lacked the bravura of a Walt Whitman. I was instead a student—even an accomplished practitioner—of bibliomancy, or divination by books. All I ever needed was the "right" book, or a library that was either big enough or eclectic enough, and I would find the way. I have always had complete confidence that the "right" book comes at the "right" time, just as the "right" person, or the teacher, comes at the "right" time, when the student is ready. I depended on dictionaries and encyclopedias far more than on maps or compasses.

In the tarot deck I would be Number IX, the Hermit Upright, making divinations from bibliomancy and omens seen on journeys.

Now it was time for a journey. Already I had traveled far, but it wasn't far enough. A Long Island debutante, a graduate of the Chapin School in New York and of Bryn Mawr College, I had come to live, twenty-one years before, in Juneau, Alaska—a most unlikely place. Here I had spent years working among people with backgrounds so different from mine that I often felt much farther away than the four thousand miles that separated me from my birthplace. For one period I worked in a statewide prison education program; for another I traveled widely for the Artists-in-the-Schools program; and I spent another year as writer-in-residence at the Alaska State Library. I had taught writing and encouraged the creative process in bars, basements, senior centers, and public gathering places throughout the state. I lived in a maelstrom of words, one filled with tentative and often short-lived beginnings; and always I was seeding that maelstrom, fanning it, whipping it up. The way out was the way in—the path of words. Magician of the alphabet, I needed only to set those twenty-six marks in motion. Now I was going to stake everything on the magic. I was going to retire from the State of Alaska, as my husband had done two years before. And we were going to set out on a long trip, spending the winter aboard our thirty-seven-foot J boat, *Monomoit*, in Antigua, in the West Indies. I was going to leave everything and everyone I knew —my job, my home, my friends, my animals, my country.

The Hermit is usually pictured as an old man standing tall and lean on top of a snowy peak. In his raised right hand he holds a lighted lantern, in his left a staff. He is looking down, with a calm sense of vision and illumination, over a wild and empty mountainscape.

That was my place, the mountainscape I had to search with the tools of divination I had at hand. That mountainscape could be where Kent had disappeared. It could also be where I would disappear.

Could I, as a writer, find the tracks of my lost colleague and his brothers and friends? Could I map the place where we all, searcher and searched, play out our lives, children in snow, making patterns both wild and beautiful that cannot be seen from the ground but only from above? I could not know, of course, until I had gone. I could make only one promise, to myself or anyone who might follow: No matter how hard it might be, it would be much harder not to go.

The Hermit Upright represents the inner search for truth and wisdom and the revelation of secrets. But reversed, he represents fear, withdrawal, loneliness, disguise, and unreasoned caution. It could go either way.

At home, I work alone at a computer in the partially finished basement of our 1920s-vintage house in downtown Juneau. Through one of two small windows I look across our front yard and the street to our neighbor's house and beyond. Bits of sky move down Gastineau Channel past Admiralty Island, past the ice-laden Taku River, past a thousand miles of mountainous coast to Seattle, our travel hub.

Where I live, there are no roads in or out; we depend

on boats and planes, and I have become keenly conscious of these means of travel. When I arrived twenty-one years ago, it was on the *Malaspina*, an Alaska state ferry named for the glacier, which is named in turn for the eighteenth-century explorer. Less than two years later, this ferry recorded a ghostly encounter.

As I look out my small window, very often the sky is gray. In winter there is little light, and the cold moves in like a lake, surrounding me in my one-armed office surplus chair, which I often share with my Abyssinian cat, Alexander. I live in fear of the cold.

Now, in May, there was nothing to do but continue watching and listening. The reports of Kent and his brothers and friends dwindled and faded, like reports coming from a distant country or from a ship moving farther and farther out of range, the voices breaking up.

I had experienced that many times on a sailboat—radio voices becoming less and less distinct. And once, in my mother-in-law's cottage in rural England, Martin and I were awakened in the middle of the night by what sounded like a deep voice coming from underwater; we could not quite make out the words. We got up and searched the house and grounds but found nothing. The next day, in the village, residents told us it was probably a drunk, but we knew no drunk could have found his way down the long winding road between the high hedgerows. And in the Revolutionary house I was brought up in, in Oyster Bay,

New York, a community of ghosts emanated from the Fleet family cemetery at the top of the hill that marked our property boundary. We lived with strange noises and occurrences. One grave, I remember from reading the epitaph, held a heart, the body having been buried at sea. As a child, I often wondered about that strange separation, about what call from the deep it would produce. Our neighbor's son vandalized the graves. Later, the neighbor himself, a disturbed man, disappeared at sea, probably a suicide.

Kent's plane went down on Sunday, May 3, about 6 P.M. The first newspaper accounts appeared on Tuesday, May 5 —the front-page story in the *Anchorage Daily News:* "Five Anglers Missing; Plane Vanishes Out of Yakutat." As a story, it was not that unusual, except for the fact that of the five men on board, three were brothers from a prominent Anchorage family: Kent Roth, thirty-seven; the pilot, Jeff Roth, forty-five; and Scott Roth, forty-four. Their two friends were Brian Barber, thirty-eight, and Tim Thornton, forty-six. Jeff was an attorney and Scott a vice president of the National Bank of Alaska. The first aircraft to respond —a Coast Guard helicopter from Cordova—began searching three hours after a scheduled radio call was missed and flew for four hours over the route filed, along the coast of the Gulf of Alaska. Monday's search focused on the Malaspina Glacier.

The May 5 papers also brought news of the first team of the spring climbing season to reach the summit of Mount

McKinley. I thought of my older son, Tom, who had summited "the Great One" just after turning eighteen.

By the next day, May 6, the story had slipped to the first page of the second, or metro, section: "Weather Slows Searchers; No Sign of Five Men Who Vanished Sunday." By then it was a story of snow, fog, and frustration. An Air Force spokesperson said, "They will search until they either find something or someone or until they exhaust all possibilities."

By May 7, the story was on the second page of the second section. Bad weather continued to hamper the search.

May 9, back on the first page of the second section, an article stated: "Volunteers asked not to crowd sky in area of search."

Many friends of the missing men, including colleagues at the Alaska Department of Fish and Game, were out looking and would continue to for weeks. They would fly their own planes, buy their fuel, go on personal time. The Alaskan Air Command Rescue Coordination Center, at Elmendorf Air Force Base, Anchorage, in charge of the search, could not handle all the volunteers.

Every lead was being checked out—reports of a hole in ice, of broken tree tops, of sun glints, of a snowslide on Mount Cook, of a duffel bag that turned out to be a ship's fender; the reports of psychics.

On May 15, back on the first page of the second section:

"11 Days and Still Searching: Fliers Scan New Areas for 5 Lost Men, Plane." The search had zeroed in on an area about one hundred miles northwest of Yakutat.

Jeff Roth, the pilot, had been flying an IFR, or Instrument Flight Rules, plan. About twenty minutes into the flight he had radioed that he was climbing to 12,000 feet. At that point, when it vanished, the plane should have been halfway across the Malaspina Glacier.

Strangely, there had been no report of trouble from the plane, nor had there been any signal from an emergency locator beacon. Now it was purely a question of how long the men, if alive on impact, could survive. A case was cited of a couple who had survived forty-nine days of Yukon winter before rescue.

The next day, May 16, it was announced that the search had been called off. It had been only twelve days. A spokesperson for the Rescue Coordination Center was quoted as saying that nearly 890 hours of flying time had been logged, covering an area larger than the state of Michigan. The rate of certainty—that nothing had been missed —was as high as 98 percent for some grids.

Publicly, the search was over. Now, increasingly, the search turned inward, its course carried by word of mouth and strength of friendship. Fish and Game employees were flying the lost plane's route. At the office, there were quiet conversations about these flights, their prospects. Collections for annual leave continued. In two months I would no

1 7

longer belong to this office, this job, these conversations, this world of relationships and connections which had been mine for the last seven years. I would be in a different world, a place I could not now see.

In my basement workspace, I got up from my chair, left the humming computer screen, and turned to the bookcase behind me, the one holding my favorite books. I pulled down the small Penguin Classics paperback *As I Crossed a Bridge of Dreams*. Since I first came upon this book—I do not remember when or how—I have felt a strange and strong connection with the nameless author, who has been given the title Lady Sarashina. A woman of eleventh-century Japan, she left a very short (eighty-page) summary of her life that is more a collage of poems and dreams than it is a narrative. What narrative there is is mostly related to pilgrimages. What she left us is gossamer: a life reflected, and caught, on the wing of a dragonfly.

In early life she lived with her family in one of Japan's most remote provinces, "beyond the end of the Great East Road." Later she went to the capital, where she was a peripheral member of the Heian court and immersed herself in poetry and fiction. There she married a civil servant (who, like her father, was sent to an eastern province) and had three children. Never content or successful in the capital, she sought escape in pilgrimages to outlying temples. These pilgrimages involved danger as well as aesthetic pleasure, especially the pleasure she took in the beauty of the landscape. She set down her travels late, when she was in her fifties and had ample distance in time and space to recollect the sadnesses of myriad separations. She then faded from the record, leaving thirty-four vignettes, which have come to be titled as they are. They constitute one of Japan's earliest travel books.

Lady Sarashina of the shades, this journey is for you. I too have lived beyond the end of the Great East Road and been stunned repeatedly by the heartbreak of separation. I too have traveled from the capital where I live, where my husband and I have worked, and recorded my expeditions in poetry and fiction. I find it hard to speak about myself. I meet you now in those spaces you left unwritten, those spaces I cannot write—and hold my lantern high. Come, let us start. It is the fifth month, a propitious time to begin. See—fiddlehead ferns are unfolding in the forests, and the tide of lupines is spreading blue across the marshlands, spreading west toward the Pacific Ocean, toward Japan.

In early June my husband and I left Juneau to fly to Massachusetts to attend the graduation of our seventeen-year-old son Sam, our youngest child, from Governor Dummer Academy.

It was a beautiful day on a beautiful campus, at the country's oldest boarding school, on the day before the event that we parents had anticipated for so long. Everything was as it should be—warm, green, lovely. Then, as we waited on the lawn after lunch, we became vaguely aware of sirens and a stirring among the clusters of soon-to-be graduates and their families. Quickly we learned the news from some students: A freshman had fallen into the Parker River, which runs at the edge of the campus, and disappeared. The afternoon froze in place. We were all—parents, grandparents, nieces and nephews, aunts, uncles, and friends, all in our baccalaureate clothes—summoned into the gymnasium and told by the tearful headmaster of the disappearance of Angel Talavera, from nearby Lawrence. "Since it has been two hours," Peter Bragdon stated, "we can only conclude he is gone." Throughout the huge room, students erupted, some screaming and running from the building, some knocking over chairs, some, like Sam beside me, going silent and rigid. Mr. Bragdon asked that an adult be with each child who left the building: None was to be alone.

We were invited to baccalaureate, now a couple of hours behind schedule. A clergyman had been hurriedly called to the nondenominational service. We followed the printed schedule, ending with "Amazing Grace." The tempo took on a rhythm beyond time, the words a meaning beyond language: I once was lost but now am found. Then there was high tea, under the green and white tent on the lawn where lunch had been served earlier. Tears spilled as we tried to talk and balance the cups of tea, the delicate cakes, the elegant food of celebration and accomplishment. Small children played on the edges. Some of us could not speak. Some of us tried to say what was deepest within us, with only partial success. By then the body had been found.

In the morning, after a radical change in the weather to wet and cold, we attended a memorial service for Angel in the chapel. Students, faculty, and staff tried to put words to the mystery. There was much I could not hear, but I did not need to. I watched as Angel's mother, barely able to walk, was supported out of the building. Passing by a dogwood in pink blossom, we immediately crossed the lawn to graduation. Sam and his classmates were in their gowns, maroon for boys and white for girls, walking to "Pomp and Circumstance." My eyes were full of tears, but I did not know whether for Angel or for these handsome young people who had accomplished so much and deserved to be happy on this, their day. My heart lay open—to the rain, which had barely held off for the ceremony, to grief, and to joy and pride, all mixed, a tumult.

On the flight back to Juneau, through four time zones, I thought of Angel, disappeared from our lives so suddenly, and of Kent. With my notebook computer, I tried to write it down, to give it a shape I could see, to make sense of it— to climb up onto that high snowy peak, lantern raised. I was at 35,000 feet, where I had spent much time in the last twenty years: the home of snow.

I had met Angel once and could not forget him. After a

poetry reading at the school, he had asked for my auto-graph—the only person ever to have done so. Angel was like that: He quickly got into your life. I had to accept his sudden exit as an ineffable mystery, one through which the universe was working in ways wise beyond my comprehension. In a way I could not know, Angel had done his work; Angel was doing his work. And Kent.

Back home, I picked up reports. The official search, Mission #920067, had been reopened on May 29 but was again limited by bad weather. It was suspended on June 5, with 924.5 hours flown in 238 sorties over 66,604.5 square miles. The unofficial search for Kent continued. A plane and pilot had been lost in that search, a not unusual occurrence. The subsearch elicited little attention in the press. The Roth family went on, driving their campaign with an energy that comes from unfathomable depths. I tried to imagine what it was for them but could not.

In medieval maps, north was equated with hope, perhaps because in the north there was so little known, so much possible. Even in the nineteenth century, the great blank expanse of the "Frozen Sea" could offer hope, because it was a place where limitations had not been set. It was a place where hope could live—the land of the mythical Hyperboreans, the "happy people" from beyond the north wind, who Pliny tells us "have long life and are famous for many marvels which border on the fabulous." Even long before Pliny, adventurous seafarers had set their sails for the misty northern islands—perhaps the Shetlands, perhaps somewhere farther. Around 300 B.C. the Greek navigator and explorer Pytheas described his voyage to Thule, that farthest northern place, situated six days' sail beyond Britain. It was, he said, a place where bread and beer could be made.

Monsters and marvels can inhabit empty spaces; but once spaces are filled—with rivers, lakes, and continents— the creations of imagination must move. Where? The Utopian lands, the Islands of the Blessed, could linger at the horizon. But when the horizon is pushed back, delineated, fixed and crowded with coordinates, then where?

Kent and his companions had fallen into that empty space beyond known latitude and longitude. It was space I needed to define, but how? How do you map disappearance? How do you say, Here! It is here! North is here! West is there! This is Truth!

Maps themselves appear and disappear. A number of famous ones have been lost for centuries. Ptolemy's *Geographia*, directions for mapmaking written in the second century, disappeared for hundreds of years, then reappeared in the fifteenth century as explorers pushed out across the globe, building on Ptolemy's rediscovered directions. It was then that Claudius Clavus, the Danish cartographer, made the first significant changes to *Geographia* by introducing the countries of the north.

The early Jesuits mapped Heaven and Hell, while the

more earthbound mapped Tenderness and the Land of Love. In *Maps and Dreams*, Hugh Brody tells us of present-day hunters in northeastern British Columbia who dream the way to heaven:

> None of this is easy to understand. But good men, the really good men, could dream of more than animals. Sometimes they saw heaven and its trails. Those trails are hard to see, and few men have had such dreams. Even if they could see dream-trails to heaven, it is hard to explain them. You draw maps of the land, show everyone where to go. You explain the hills, the rivers, the trails from here to Hudson Hope, the roads. Maybe you make maps of where the hunters go and where the fish can be caught. That is not easy. But easier, for sure, than drawing out the trails to heaven. You may laugh at these maps of the trails to heaven, but they were done by the good men who had the heaven dream, who wanted to tell the truth. They worked hard on their truth.

Maps can be made of anything: sticks, stone, sand. Skin, silver, computer printout. They can be of any shape—in the beginning, round; as they moved into books, square and rectangular, sometimes in the shape of a heart, but always flat; now, digitized, in Braille, on-screen. They can be made from any perspective, used for any bias, for any purpose, but they can never be totally objective. North, that place of hope, has come to be on top; many maps, as a result, lack the depiction of a compass.

I had to know where I stood. Only then could I begin to look for someone else. Only then could I begin to find the truth.

I was born in New York in April 1942. On my mother's side, I am Irish; on my father's side, English and Huguenot—a curious combination, since the Huguenots fled to America to escape the Catholics. Within the western zodiac, I am Aries; within the Chinese, Horse. I am among the very few exceptions in my family to have left the metropolitan New York area. I remember my grandmother—my father's mother—telling the story of some hapless cousins who had gone west, I think to Illinois: Money was sent, but the land was sold off, and when relatives visited, they found bathroom fixtures sitting in the front yard.

CHAPTER III

Lituya Bay: Guardian of the Gulf

Where I stood, physically, in Juneau, Alaska, was close to the search area. Yakutat lies approximately two hundred miles to the northwest. In my twenty years in Juneau, I had flown over the area many times in Boeing 737s—sometimes in clear weather, sometimes in stormy, and quite often in turbulence. Once I had flown over it, or a fragment of it, in a 1942 amphibious Grumman Widgeon, sightseeing from Glacier Bay inland around Mount Fairweather, over to Lituya Bay and down the coast to outer Chichagof Island. Buddy Ferguson piloted me and Martin, Sam, and our nephew Conan. Both boys were airsick. I liked being in a wonderful plane as old as I was, swooping down onto the

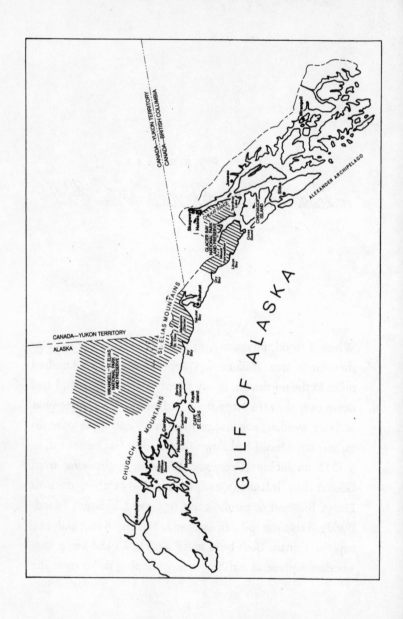

surface of the water for landings and takeoffs, a wall of water and a great roar upfront.

The Gulf of Alaska is a crescent of wild, unprotected water where the compass moves erratically and the shores consist of massive mountains straddling volatile plates. From Cross Sound in the south to Prince William Sound in the north, there are few harbors—Lituya Bay, Dry Bay, Yakutat Bay, Icy Bay, and Controller Bay. These indentations, though providing some protection from the open water, give way to a wildness every bit as great—the huge glaciers, icefields, and mountains of the Fairweather, St. Elias, and Chugach ranges. A backdrop to much of this area is the huge and rugged wilderness of the Wrangell–St. Elias, largest of all U.S. national parks. From these mountains boils weather every bit as volatile as the geotectonics under their restless roots. More shipwrecks have occurred along this coast than any other coast in Alaska.

Foremost among these weather-making mountains are Mount Fairweather (15,300 feet), near Lituya Bay, and Mount St. Elias (18,008 feet), to the north, near Icy Bay. Behind Mount St. Elias rises Mount Logan (19,850 feet), the highest mountain in Canada and the second highest in North America, after Mount McKinley (20,320 feet). Within the Wrangell–St. Elias National Park and Preserve, four peaks top 16,000 feet. Mount Wrangell (14,163 feet) is the highest active volcano in the state.

From the water, the peaks of Mount Fairweather and

Mount St. Elias dominate the wildly beautiful mountain-scape and broadcast the nature of the weather—the weather that gets trapped as it tries to move east from the gulf. Tlingit legend holds that once these two peaks were married but that they separated during a family quarrel. St. Elias, the man, traveled west, taking slaves and men with him; these represent the mountains between the two larger ones. The mountains to the east of Fairweather are the couple's children.

These mountains, perhaps the last place on earth that Kent saw, have a recent history also of separation and loss. Our first account of them comes from the Bering-Chirikov expedition, the ill-fated Russian voyage of two hundred years ago that brought Europeans and the original inhabitants of Alaska together for the first time.

Soon after setting off from Kamchatka on June 4, 1741, Vitus Bering, on the *St. Peter*, became separated from his second-in-command, Aleksei Chirikov, on the *St. Paul*. Miscommunication, fog, and storm were the probable causes. The two mariners were never to see each other again. America would be "found" independently within a day of each other by two men who were lost to each other and separated forever. Their double discovery came through disappearance.

On July 15, off southeast Alaska, latitude 55°21′, Chirikov became the first to sight land. The next day, to the north, Bering sighted land—the St. Elias Range, near Yakutat.

On July 17, Chirikov anchored at 57°15′, in a bay off the north end of what we now know as Chichagof Island, probably in the vicinity of Lisiansky Strait. He dispatched a longboat with the mate and ten armed sailors. The boat never returned. On the twenty-third, a second boat was sent in search of the first, and that too disappeared, though two canoes filled with Natives appeared the following day. After several days of agonized waiting, Chirikov gave up hope for his men. Without any landing boats, and with his numbers seriously depleted, he deemed it best to return to Kamchatka without further attempt at landfall. No clue to either missing boat was ever found. Historians and ethnographers since have not been able to conclude whether the men were killed by the local Tlingit Indians or drowned in the powerful riptides.

Bering, in the meantime, was sailing north of his partner. He saw and noted Mount St. Elias, though he did not name it; he named nearby Cape St. Elias. To the north, he made landfall on Kayak Island, in Controller Bay, just south of Prince William Sound. Kayak Island faces the massive glacier now named for Bering.

This glacier, the longest glacier in North America and the second largest, reaches 125 miles back into the Chugach Mountains. Combined with the vast Bagley icefield, from which it flows, it covers approximately 2,250 square miles, for the overall largest mass of ice. According to scientists, the Bering Glacier is in a retreat phase, which causes giant icebergs to break off into the Gulf of Alaska, endangering shipping; that shipping includes tankers moving oil from the pipeline terminus at Valdez, in Prince William Sound.

South and east of the Bering Glacier and just north of Yakutat streams the frozen river of the Malaspina Glacier, the continent's largest. A piedmont glacier, it rises from the foot of Mount St. Elias and travels beyond the mountain valley to level land, covering approximately 850 square miles between Yakutat Bay and Icy Bay. Its size is often compared to that of Rhode Island. Fed by more than twenty-five smaller glaciers, its whole complex covers an area of approximately 2,000 square miles.

Either of these glaciers could have claimed Kent and his plane. A crevasse could have swallowed them like the trough of a storm-whipped frozen sea, a crevasse quickly filled with layer upon layer of snow.

Most volatile of all the places along this seething coast is Lituya Bay, fierce spirit of the gulf. Lituya Bay (meaning, in Tlingit, "Lake at the Point") is a place where fire and ice struggle to shape the tortured land. The head of the T-shaped bay, lying directly over the Fairweather fault, which separates the North American and the Pacific plates, is a ragged landscape where earthquakes, avalanches, and landslides have frequently scarred the rock face. Site of at least five giant waves, Lituya Bay has a history as scarred as its terrain.

Oral history and legend suggest why no one has lived at the bay for many years. Its fearsome spirits finally got the better of human inhabitants. The chief force, according to one of its earliest chroniclers, George Thornton Emmons, was the Spirit of Lituya Bay,

> a monster of the deep who dwells in the ocean caverns near the entrance. He is known as Kah Lituya, "the Man of Lituya." He resents any approach to his domain, and all of those whom he destroys become his slaves, and take the form of bears, and from their watchtowers on the lofty mountains of the Mount Fairweather range they herald the approach of canoes, and with their master they grasp the surface water and shake it as if it were a sheet, causing tidal waves to rise and engulf the unwary.

According to Tlingit stories, Land Otter Men, or Kooshdaka, also haunt the area, as they do all the southeastern coast. Listening for the calls of those who are drowning or those who are lost in the woods, Land Otter Men are ready to "rescue" these unfortunate beings and take them to their own shadowy world. If the victims are not rescued by a shaman, they cannot return.

There was much that Native residents had to fear. And more was to come with the advent of the white men.

Though Captain James Cook and various Russian explorers sailed the coast of southeast Alaska and some of the Russians might have entered Lituya Bay, the first European we know to have visited the bay was the French explorer Comte de La Pérouse.

On July 3, 1786, with his two ships, *L'Astrolabe* and *La Boussole,* La Pérouse began what was to be a new chapter in the dramatic history of one of Alaska's most violent places. On a voyage around the world, he was as well equipped as anyone could be in the late eighteenth century for scientific studies. He left us, fortunately, a full account of his activities and his relationships with the Natives he encountered.

It was a visit of disaster. Before La Pérouse arrived, there had recently been a mass drowning of local Tlingit inhabitants, and the people were mourning and wary. La Pérouse's entry into the bay was not auspicious. "During the thirty years that I have followed the sea I never saw two vessels so near being lost," he commented.

On July 13, ten days after he anchored, La Pérouse lost two longboats with a total of twenty-one men and officers in the riptide. On July 22, a group of Tlingits came to him with fragments of one of the lost boats and indicated they had found one of the bodies. Three of the officers followed the Indians, paying them along the way in response to demands. After seven or eight miles, the Indians vanished into the woods. They may have found a body, but, fearful of the Spirit of Lituya Bay and of Land Otter Men, they had not secured it.

La Pérouse stayed on for two weeks in case any survivors might show up. Like Chirikov, who lost two boats with fifteen men not far to the south in 1741, La Pérouse was loath to leave. To commemorate the loss, he placed a wooden monument on the island in the middle of the bay, which he had purchased from the Natives and which he came to name Isle du Cenotaphe. The monument read, "Reader, whoever thou art, mingle thy tears with ours."

When La Pérouse finally sailed away, saddened by his loss and embittered by bickerings with the Natives, it was to his own disappearance. He looked for the mythical Jardines in the Marianas, but could not find them. In September 1787, he followed instructions to find another mythical, and reportedly valuable, island, Rica de Plata. On giving up that search, he turned south. In January 1788 he got to Botany Bay, Australia, the last place he was heard from. It was not until 1826 that Captain Peter Dillon found La Pérouse's sword, at Vanikoro, in the Santa Cruz group. Two years later one of his anchors and some of his guns were found. The discovery of sixty skulls indicated that he and his men had been cannibalized. In the meantime, King Louis XVI, who had launched the expedition, had lost his own head.

La Pérouse's journals were carried from Kamchatka overland to Paris and to the safety of publication; that journey alone was nearly nine thousand treacherous miles. A glacier was later named in honor of La Pérouse. The only glacier that feeds directly into the open water of the Pacific Ocean, it runs down from Mount La Pérouse, at the southern end of the Fairweather Range, and lies about fifteen miles south of Lituya Bay. A variable name is Desolation Glacier—and for the bay, Frenchman's Bay.

After La Pérouse, a quick succession of explorers visited the surrounding coast and the area of Yakutat Bay: the British mariners Dixon and Colnett, and the Russians Ismailov and Bocharov, who visited Lituya Bay in 1788, finding artifacts from La Pérouse's expedition. In 1791, a significant visit to the coast was made by Alejandro Malaspina and José Bustamente y Guerra, Spanish navy officers, who assembled a large ethnographic collection. Because of the disfavor Malaspina fell into when he returned to Spain, however, much of what he took back, including notes and maps, was scattered and lost. The Tlingits of southeast Alaska still don't know what was taken from them by the masters of the *Descubierta* (Discovery) and *Atrevida* (Daring).

After Malaspina, most of the activity along the gulf coast was that of Russian entrepreneurs in the sea otter trade. In 1805, the subjugated Tlingits revolted at Yakutat and destroyed the agricultural settlement the Russians had been attempting to establish, known as New Russia. Soon after, three hundred Natives were lost in a storm at sea. The Russian settlement was never reestablished.

In the meantime, it became impossible to inhabit Lituya Bay. The great wave of 1853 or 1854 is said to have destroyed all life in the bay. Aside from the men who were out hunting, only one woman escaped. She had been picking berries and, unlike the others in her party, did not try to rush back to the village. Afterward, no attempt at permanent habitation was made in the area.

At least five major waves have ripped through Lituya Bay since 1853, when the Tlingits left it for good. The waves of 1936 and 1958 are the best known. Other cataclysmic waves occurred in 1874 and 1899. The series of earthquakes that occurred in September 1899, which shook the area for eight days, elevated part of the shore of Yakutat Bay, to the north, by forty-seven feet.

Few people have attempted to live there since the Tlingits abandoned it. The gold rush brought some hearty prospectors, but few of them prospered. An unusual event occurred in the winter of 1899–1900. Hannah and Hans Nelson had moved to the bay the previous summer with three single men to find gold. Trapped by cold weather, with little food, the party faced a grim winter. Perhaps overcome by strain, one of the three men shot another to death and tried to kill the third man as well as the Nelsons. The survivors restrained him, held him, and, unable to get the local Tlingits to transport him to Juneau, tried and executed him in as formal a procedure as could be effected—an example of frontier justice. The incident was later embellished and made famous by Jack London in his story "The Unexpected." In the fictional account, it is Mrs. Nelson who does the hanging.

Although placer miners continued to inhabit the bay in an irregular fashion, washing gold from its glacial deposits, there was only one longtime inhabitant. A hermit, Jim Huscroft, moved into the bay in 1917 and built a cabin on Cenotaph Island, where La Pérouse had erected his memorial for the twenty-one lost men. Huscroft trapped foxes until they were gone, fished, hunted goats, and grew a large garden. He barely survived the wave of 1936, which removed some of his buildings, destroyed his garden, and reached into his cabin. Defeated and in poor health, he was never quite the same after that. His health continued to deteriorate. Finally, in March 1939, a friend, Osa Nolde, took him out to Juneau to get medical attention. On the way a storm drove them to the Gunk Hole, Elfin Cove, where Huscroft died aboard his friend's boat—the *Cenotaph*. He was buried later on Long Island, near Hoonah, as the weather was much too stormy to return his remains to Lituya Bay. The mountaineer Bradford Washburn provided a bronze plaque, later bolted to a rock on Cenotaph Island, acknowledging Huscroft's assistance with the Dartmouth Alaskan expeditions of 1930, 1932, 1933, and 1934.

Huscroft's diaries fared worse than the journals of the great explorer who first visited the bay. Of the numerous volumes, only one has been found, by the historian of Lituya Bay, Francis Caldwell. That diary turned up in an old fishing boat in Juneau. The fate of the other volumes is uncertain; they might have been discarded over time by those who did not recognize their value, or destroyed by ransackers searching the dead man's cabin for a cache of gold. They might still be found.

Huscroft died well before the next cataclysm. In July 1958, three boats were anchored in the bay when an earthquake measuring 7.8 on the Richter scale contorted the Fairweather Range and hurled 90 million tons of rock into the water. In the west arm of the T-shaped bay, part of the mountainside slid into the water, creating a wave that tore more than seventeen hundred feet up the opposite slope. Smaller waves followed. One of the three boats disappeared with all on board; a second was sunk outside the bay, but the crew was rescued; the third rode out the cataclysm. Jim Huscroft's cabin and what was left of his garden were swept away. His monument remains.

From the time La Pérouse sailed with such hazard into the bay, the history of the area has been one of impact and change. While the great waves of water have played their part, other waves have rolled over the land. Disease, in particular, took a great toll.

Smallpox was perhaps introduced by the Spanish expedition of 1775, when Cuadra took the *Sonora* as far north as fifty-eight degrees, near Cross Sound. Well established in southeast Alaska by the 1780s, the disease broke out in a severe epidemic in Sitka in 1836. By 1840, half the Tlingit population of the region had died. Another epidemic raged in 1862. There were also outbreaks of measles and typhoid, then syphilis, brought by the Russians. Epidemics raged to the north as well. The smallpox epidemic of 1838–39 may have claimed 60 percent of the Bristol Bay and Kuskokwim population.

In the meantime, waves of missionaries swept north along the coast, wrestling with spirit. Gold miners and mountain climbers invaded, assaulting the terrain, while the U.S. Navy attempted to keep order. On the water, the search for the depleted sea otters gave way to the search for whales, and the maritime traffic increased.

In 1886, Lieutenant Frederick Schwatka, who had been involved in the epic search for the lost Franklin expedition, led the *New York Times* expedition in its attempt on Mount St. Elias, the point of land Vitus Bering first saw in America, the mountain that had quarreled with its mate and moved west, the point of land that, perhaps, Kent had last seen. The group, which included the well-known Princeton professor Dr. William Libbey, did not succeed. The mountain was finally conquered in 1897 by Prince Luigi Amadeo, duke of Abruzzi, who also made an unsuccessful run at the

North Pole. Mount Fairweather, a smaller but equally difficult challenge, was not scaled until 1931.

Finally, during World War II, the U.S. Army settled into Yakutat. Domination of the Gulf of Alaska was complete. Its indigenous people, stripped of citizenship, entered a political realm of the living dead—a political Kingdom of the Land Otter Men. Native influence was decimated, Native history forgotten. If not for the arduous scholarship of a few, particularly George Thornton Emmons and Frederica de Laguna, and now Richard and Nora Dauenhauer, it would have largely disappeared. In all of that vast area that was once Tlingit domain, one of the few Indian names extant is that of Lituya Bay. It is as if Lituya Bay, with its innate power and its fearsome history, could alone transcend the invasions, throwing off each new attempt.

The Spirit of Lituya Bay and the Land Otter Men rule yet. The giant bears haunt the coast. When you fly low over the coast near Lituya Bay today, you see them foraging in the salmon-rich streams. All of an enormous size, they range from dark to honey-colored. And numerous are the disappearances in that untamed, unanswering land.

Native carvers sometimes depict the Tlingit legend of the Lady of Lituya Bay: A band of Tlingits once raided the bay in an overland attack, killing many victims. They took a woman hostage to guide them safely out of the dangerous waters of the bay. The woman, grieving for her slain husband and family, directed the raiding party onto shoals, killing them all—and herself in the process.

My place—my life—was Lituya Bay: beautiful, breaking open, scarred; crisscrossed with echoes and ghosts; a place dangerous to enter and leave.

Soon after graduating from college, I married Martin, the boy next door, and we left immediately for Boulder, Colorado. Martin, after earning a degree in history, was to study civil engineering. Then, after two degrees, it was time to move on. In Colorado, I gave birth to Helen, in 1965, and Tom, in 1968, and worked at a variety of jobs, from news editor of an insolvent weekly paper to editor of theoretical astrophysics at the Joint Institute for Laboratory Astrophysics. I began and dropped out of graduate school and took a night course on how to publish what you write. I said to myself, I will publish poetry. If by the fiftieth attempt I have not succeeded, I will give it up. I had forty-nine rejections before my first acceptance.

CHAPTER IV
Search for the Soul

Many come to Alaska searching. Almost invariably, those who come to Alaska, the land of promise, come to find that which is lost only to themselves—money, power, position, authority—or a wilderness they think will save them from the evils of a more crowded world. They come with hope, because the spaces within Alaska are very large and the unnamed peaks of mountains and the unnamed glaciers many. The horizon, often obscured by range after range of rock—or of fog—has not quite been pinned down. Boundaries are vague. Coordinates are pliable or nonexistent. Vestiges of the Utopian, or Hyperborean, legend remain: There might just be a place, a place of new beginnings, a place beyond hassle, where satisfaction can be had, and riches; a place, indeed, "famous for many marvels which border on the fabulous."

At the North Pole (as at the South), all lines of longitude merge, and there is only one direction. And that direction is never quite certain. The magnetic pole, far from the geographic one, moves constantly. With the earth wobbling on its axis, the geographic pole moves too; and who can be really certain of its location? When Robert E. Peary reached it in April 1909, or thought he had, he traveled several miles in every direction out from it to make sure he could assert his claim.

Into this place of moving quest many have come to project their map. From the first mention of the Strait of Anian by Marco Polo, cartographers and explorers of the north have come, seeking a route to riches. That strait, undoubtedly what we now know as Bering Strait, represented not only a separation between Asia and North America but also a means to connect the two and find wealth in the process. It was the route to exploitation.

Wave after wave of searchers, seekers, have come to Alaska—first looking for a northwest passage to India that would enable trade with the East and boost the flagging English wool industry; then for the pelts of sea otters and fur seals to enrich the coffers of Russian merchants; then for whales and fish; now for oil, minerals, trees, and what is left of the fish. These waves loop over the map, rising and falling and intersecting, a moving set of meridians and parallels. They disappear into history books and tales of loss. Resource after resource disappears with them, as do those who go in pursuit. I had come that way myself, in 1971, with my family, in search of jobs and opportunity. We thought, as the license plates then declared, "North to the Future."

It is a search that started early in the history of what was to become Alaska and a search that continues in a land struggling to know itself beneath the tourist hype and hope. It pulls us up to and across the empty spaces—naming, claiming, pressing on. There, just on the horizon—now blocked by a mountain peak, now by a storm—is the place we always knew existed, and it is ours. We will shape it to our expectations. We will make it ours.

Soon after the United States bought Alaska from Russia, in 1867, the pivotal point of conflict between the new American officials and the indigenous people became the shaman. The shaman was the liaison between earth and heaven, the seen and the unseen, the intercessionary between human and divine—the cause of cure, weather, and good hunting. As long as the people believed in the shamans and their inexplicable power, they could not be controlled. The clash was inevitable.

During the 1880s and 1890s, the authorities in southeast Alaska were officers of the U.S. Navy. These officials were determined to break the power of the shamans. The danger, they stated, lay in how shamans, attempting a cure, denounced certain people as witches. George Thornton Emmons, the well-known and generally accurate ethnographer of the Tlingit people, served as a Navy officer in southeast Alaska in the 1880s and 1890s and himself shows the bias typical of his peers:

> When the chant, dance, and hocus-pocus failed to cure, the shaman denounced someone for charming or bewitching his patient, and demanded his torture or death. Usually the infirm or the aged poor, slaves or personal enemies, were denounced and subjected to fiendish tortures. Captain E. C. Merriman, U.S.N., broke the power of shamanism in the archipelago by repeated rescues of those charged with witchcraft, by fine and punishment of tribe and shamans, and finally by taking the shamans on board his ship, shaving off and burning their long sacred hair and sending them out bald-headed, to be met with roars of Tlingit laughter. There have been few cases of witchcraft since.

Commanders Beardslee, Glass, and Lull also contended with the problem, as did William T. Burwell, commander of the *Pinta*, as late as 1893. Numerous accounts tell of the seizing of shamans and the cutting of their hair. In one case, a shorn shaman had his head painted with red lead.

In the meantime, while the Navy was exerting the power of the nation, Christian missionaries were beginning to move throughout southeast Alaska exerting the power of a joyless Presbyterian god. They too focused on the evil deeds of shamans who accused "victims" of witchcraft. The shamans, of course, were simply the visible sign, the lightning rod catching the storm. The vengeful god of the Old Testament was loosed on Alaska in his fury.

Horrible tortures of accused witches were recorded by the missionaries S. Hall Young in Wrangell and Caroline Willard in Haines. These consisted largely of the victim's being bound in an extremely painful manner, thrust into a dark hole under a house, whipped with devil's club, and starved.

Young, who came to Wrangell in 1878 (and who traveled with John Muir), faced down the shamans, when he could, and freed the victims. He wrote: "I firmly believe that all of the medicine-men in Southeastern Alaska at that time and since were *conscious frauds*. They were in the business simply for the profit that there was in it. They did not believe in their own powers." The truth of it was, Young was the vanguard of the Presbyterian phalanx just entering Alaska in search of the Native soul.

Beaten back, the shamans of Wrangell desisted. Young claimed that at one point there were "seven girls and six boys in our school under our care, who had been accused, and in some cases tied up, as witches," but who had escaped to the refuge of Wrangell. There was more to follow.

In 1877, a year earlier, the Presbyterian Board of Missions had sent Mrs. A. R. McFarland and the Reverend

Sheldon Jackson to Wrangell as teachers and missionaries. Within five years Sitka and Haines were part of the Presbyterian realm as well. Jackson, appointed general agent of education for Alaska in 1885, was then able to assume civil as well as church authority in his efforts to capture the soul of the territory. The map he would make was a Christian map. Although it was not to replicate the very early maps based on the body of Christ, with Jerusalem at its center, its purpose was the same. The vast reaches of Alaska would belong to Jesus Christ.

Under Jackson's direction, the Moravians settled into Bethel, on the Kuskokwim River, in 1885, and the Episcopalians claimed Anvik, on the Yukon River, in 1887, the same year the Roman Catholics, working independently, set up their mission at Holy Cross, downriver from the Episcopalians. In 1890 the Episcopalians settled into Point Hope, the Congregational Church at Wales, and the Presbyterian Church at Barrow; and seven years later, the Quakers at Kotzebue. The more generous-spirited Russian Orthodox priests were gone, but they would not be forgotten.

Throughout the different Christian creeds and rituals established in the territory by 1900 ran one common thread essential to the Sheldon Jackson plan: The Alaska Native had to be educated to the white man's way; his morality, his ethics, his hygiene, his clothing, his housing, his language, his way of life, had to conform. There was no place for the wild-haired shaman, who disappeared with his mask and his rattle into the woods, the tundra, the ice. The shaman, in Jackson's writings, is associated with greed, debauchery, slavery, even cannibalism—some ate human flesh, while others ate the flesh of dogs, he said. In short, the shaman was the devil of the north.

Hidden roots of shamanism would settle into the earth, keeping alive like a fungus, but the flower—the mask-wearing, drum-beating ritual—was gone. We are left with snatches of oral history, much of it collected in southeast Alaska by Emmons and by the contemporary Bryn Mawr College anthropologist Frederica de Laguna, who has recently edited Emmons's work. The accounts are infused with a power that was beyond understanding but also a part of everyday life. It was everywhere and could not be questioned, and it was great enough to have frightened the missionaries and the naval officers. It was a power beyond oceans, continents, and coastlines, a power that knew no limits, no latitude or longitude. It was a power beyond life itself, and it bound heaven and earth.

Accidentally coming upon a dead shaman's grave could cause death or serious illness. With proper pay, the shaman could summon his spirits and send them far and wide to find a hunter who was lost, soul-travel to a distant place to secure news of others, perform a cure or help with a difficult childbirth, bring fish or game when they were lacking, or save someone from the evil spell of witches and Land Otter Men.

To the shaman, the greatest enemy was the witch, the evildoer who brought illness, misery, and death to his or her victim. It was the witch with whom the shaman was locked in combat, and the witch who was to be the shaman's downfall.

Another entity greatly feared was the Land Otter, or Kooshdaka. Land Otter Men were known as a race of supernatural beings in human form, or transformed human beings. They "saved" or captured those who drowned or were lost in the woods and took them to their shadowy homes under the earth, where the otters were disguised as people. Unless the unfortunate victims were saved by a shaman, they too became land otters, unable to return to their human world.

Children were especially vulnerable. It was said that land otters wanted to capture human beings because people were killing so many land otters. It was an enmity of long duration. Even today Kooshdaka is feared, and stories are told of mysterious appearances and disappearances in the watery and stormy coastlands of southeast Alaska. A drowning person who calls for help and a disoriented person alone in the woods are in terrible danger. Kooshdaka is ever present, waiting and listening. Kooshdaka hungers for the human soul.

But a shaman, calling in powers to help him or her, can match the strength of Kooshdaka or a witch. And the shaman can do much more. One female shaman of Controller Bay (where Vitus Bering made his landing on Kayak Island) is said to have brought back to life her two young sons, who had been stabbed to death. Another shaman made her brother an invincible hunter and predicted the coming of the Russians. A famous shaman sent his spirit to locate a hunter who was missing and cured a man who had been mauled by a bear. This same shaman was famed for traveling in his soul from Yakutat to Sitka to check on two women there whose relatives were worried about them. When he "returned," he said that one of the women was crying because her child had died. In the spring, when the people from Sitka came to Yakutat in their canoes, the first thing they said was, "Your Indian doctor came over to Sitka. One of the women was crying. The Indian doctor saw it."

Far from southeast Alaska in the Arctic, the Danish ethnographer Knud Rasmussen was among the last to have contact with significant shamans, during his trek across North America in the Fifth Thule Expedition, 1921–24. Rasmussen committed to paper some of the last words of a vanishing age, spoken by those who could commune with the power of the universe.

One of these was the great *angakoq*, or shaman, Igjugarjuk of the Caribou Eskimos of Lake Hikoligjuaq, with whom Rasmussen traveled briefly. (The general term "Eskimo" is used as cited in historical texts. Modern references, where appropriate, are to Inupiat Eskimos, residents of northern and northwestern parts of Alaska, and Yupik Eskimos, residents of southwest Alaska. The term "Native" refers to an indigenous resident of the area.) Igjugarjuk, chief of the Willow Tribe, was widely known for his powers. According to him, "All true wisdom is only to be learned far from the dwellings of men, out in the great solitudes; and is only to be attained through suffering. Privation and suffering are the only things that can open the mind of man to those things which are hidden from others."

Rasmussen relates how Igjugarjuk initiated two people into the powers of shamanism. One was Kinalik, the shaman's sister-in-law, who was hung on tent poles for five days in severe winter weather, then shot with a stone loaded into a gun. Another was Aggjartoq, who was lashed to a pole, carried to a lake, thrust in through a hole cut in the ice, and kept standing on the bottom of the lake, his head under water, for five days. When he was pulled up, his clothes showed no sign of being wet.

As Rasmussen notes: "These inland Eskimos are very little concerned about the idea of death; they believe that all men are born again, the soul passing on continually from one form of life to another. Good men return to earth as men, but evildoers are reborn as beasts, and in this way the earth is replenished, for no life once given can ever be lost or destroyed."

It is these inland, or Caribou, Eskimos whom Farley Mowat was to write about fifty years later in *People of the Deer* and *The Desperate People*, portraying a lost tribe demoralized by government interference and misuse and on the verge of an agonizing extinction. Already Rasmussen had thought he had arrived a hundred years too late to capture the essence of the shaman. He found Igjugarjuk listening to Caruso records on a gramophone, his people eating tinned food—"the worst kind of tinpot store and canned provision culture."

In 1924, at the end of his trek from east to west across the frozen top of North America, Rasmussen came to Nome, where he found the last shaman he was to encounter —Najagneq, from Nunivak Island. Najagneq had just been released from a year in the Nome jail, where he had been kept on charges of murder until the case against him evaporated for want of witnesses. Rasmussen closes with the words of Najagneq, speaking of the great power of the universe in which he believed—

a power that we call Sila, which is not to be explained in simple words. A great spirit, supporting the world and the weather and all life on earth, a spirit so mighty that his utterance to mankind is not through common words, but by storm and snow and rain and the fury of the sea; all the forces of nature that men fear. But he has also another way of utterance, by sunlight, and calm of the sea, and little children innocently at play. . . . No one has seen Sila; his place of being is a mystery, in that he is at once among us and unspeakably far away.

From the beginning of their tenure in what was to become Alaska, the Russian Orthodox priests had had the wisdom not to interfere with the shamans. Unlike the Protestants and the Roman Catholics, who followed them, they felt no need for assimilation. The people, in turn, saw much of the Orthodox ritual as similar to that of their shamans. The priests' laissez-faire attitude allowed Orthodoxy to take root more deeply than might have been expected. In some places it far outlasted priests and active churches.

There was not always complete acceptance and peace, however. In their earliest years the Russian missionaries found trouble. The Very Reverend Michael Oleksa, of the Russian Orthodox Church, has done exhaustive research to explain one of the great murder mysteries of Alaska, that of the priest-monk Juvenaly (Iakov Fedorovich Govoruchkin), who disappeared in the vicinity of Lake Iliamna in 1796. As one of the first Orthodox missionaries to arrive in Alaska, in 1793, Juvenaly had traveled widely, making converts in the Yakutat and Prince William Sound areas and in large areas north of Kodiak and west of Kenai. A churchman who advocated that Native Alaskans should have the same basic civil rights as Russian citizens, he was loathed by both Baranov and Rezanov, the managers of what would become the Russian-American Company.

When Juvenaly disappeared, Baranov wrote that he had been killed by the Natives of the Lake Iliamna area because of their distrust of him and his brutality. The famous chronicler of eighteenth- and nineteenth-century Alaska, Hubert Bancroft, made use of what later turned out to be a bogus diary of the missionary to explain his disappearance in similarly unflattering terms: Juvenaly had allowed himself to be seduced by an Iliamna woman and had lost the respect of the people. Oral tradition of the Kuskokwim area revealed, however, a very different story: that Juvenaly was instantly killed by Natives in the area of Quinhagak when he arrived and rose in his boat to preach. Seeing the cross on his chest, local inhabitants assumed it represented a spiritual power against which they had to defend themselves. Juvenaly died a martyr.

In Father Oleksa's words,

for nearly two centuries the circumstances of Hieromonk Juvenaly's death have been obscured by misinformation, deliberate slander, forgery and anti-clerical propaganda. Upon further investigation of all reliable original source materials and analysis of later reports filed by explorers and missionaries, together with the unanimous and consistent oral tradition of the indigenous peoples of the region, it now appears that

Father Juvenaly died as a martyr for the Faith on the western shores of Alaska, near the present site of the village of Quinhagak.

No remains have yet been found. Interestingly, in the Iliamna area, oral tradition provides the story of a priest, barefoot and in the snow, running for his life into the mountains to the north; on reaching the edge of a cliff, his tracks simply disappeared. It is a place where strange tales of monsters and marvels are told even today.

The potential for conflict between churchman and shaman was always present. Sometimes an epidemic was the battlefield. Sometimes white man's medicine won out against the shaman's. Sometimes not, or not entirely.

As the Tlingits saw it, epidemics came by boat. Only the shaman could see the boat of death coming. According to de Laguna, "In this 'Canoe of Sickness' the shaman can see the ghosts of those who had died of fever, perhaps those who had died in Sitka if the epidemic were spreading from there, and he would try to drive the boat away." In this case, the shamans were to prove remarkably prophetic; the diseases carried by the Canoes of Sickness, including alcoholism, were to prove devastating to Alaska Natives, as well as to indigenous peoples throughout the Americas.

During the great smallpox epidemics of the 1800s, Russian officials had the opportunity to make use of vaccines. Sometimes, when enough of the Native population accepted vaccines, the white man's medicine revealed a power far greater than that of the shaman, and in the view of the people, the shaman was vanquished. In Sitka, a number of Tlingits even converted to Christianity after seeing the difference between the results of the Russians' medicine and the shaman's medicine when it came to the virulence of smallpox.

In 1890, as shamans, Orthodoxy, and the new Moravian missionaries struggled for the soul of the Kuskokwim, an epidemic of a different sort—one of "insanity"—gripped the villages near Bethel, culminating in the bloody murder of a Yupik Moravian convert known as Brother Hooker. John Kilbuck was a Moravian missionary who served many years in the area with his wife, Edith. In his words, a possible explanation may be "that the crisis of the conflict between the Gospel and the powers of evil—proved too much for the minds of these simple minded Eskimos. —The strain was undoubtedly great—for the shamans were active—and so were the Greeks—and the missionaries. —The shamans stood up for Diana of the Ephesians— and the Greeks for the tradition of the fathers—and both combined against the New Way."

In 1898, Kilbuck, through admissions of adultery, lost his standing in the church and was dismissed. When Ernest and Caroline Weber, the Kilbucks' replacements, attempted to reach the Kuskokwim, however, they were lost in a storm at sea.

John and Edith moved to Quinhagak and continued the work of the Moravian Church. The next winter, suffering blood poisoning, John had to undergo an amputation of his right arm. The loss of his arm in such a manner increased his stature among the Natives. He became the subject of legend.

In the spring of 1900, news of a further incidence of adultery on John's part led to his dismissal from the church. He went to work for the Census Bureau, only to be immersed in the deadly 1900 epidemic of influenza along the Kuskokwim—the "great sickness," as it is still referred to. Later the Kilbucks moved to Barrow to work as teachers for the U.S. Bureau of Education, and then to Wainwright, and finally to Douglas, across the channel from Juneau. They returned to the Kuskokwim in 1911.

By the time Kilbuck lived down his sin and returned to the Kuskokwim, the war with the shaman was over. The white man's way had flooded the state, aided in no small measure by the waves of deadly disease. Within another generation, no one in Alaska would be openly referred to as a shaman. The secret power went underground. The quest for Alaska's soul was almost achieved.

The church crisscrossed the state—by dogsled, by canoe, by powerboat, by snowshoe, and later by snow-machine and airplane. It reached to the most remote areas. A churchman, indeed, led the first successful assault on Mount McKinley, the continent's highest peak, in the heart of the Territory of Alaska. Hudson Stuck, Episcopal archdeacon of the Yukon, organized the historic climb of 1913, though it was his twenty-year-old protégé, Walter Harper, who actually was first to the top.

Harper's father was Irish, the first miner in the Yukon; his mother, Athabaskan. At sixteen, Harper became Stuck's companion, assistant, and student. After the climb, Stuck sent the young man to Mt. Hermon School in Massachusetts, where he spent three years. Upon his return, he and Stuck made a trip of approximately two thousand miles by dogsled from Fort Yukon to Kotzebue and up along the coast to Barrow, then back to Fort Yukon.

In September 1918, Harper married Frances Wells, a nurse at Fort Yukon. They decided to leave the territory to pursue war work and, eventually, medical school for Walter. On October 22, in Skagway, they boarded the last ship out of the north before winter, the *Princess Sophia*. That night the *Sophia* foundered on Vanderbilt Reef, near Juneau. On October 25, in a violent storm, the ship slipped off the reef. The rescue ships that had ringed the stricken vessel had to withdraw. All 343 men, women, and children aboard perished, most suffocated by oil or overcome by hypothermia. The Harpers were buried in Juneau. Hudson Stuck saw that they were given a fitting monument, that they were not lost in Evergreen Cemetery in the capital. Harper "has left behind him," Stuck wrote, "a sweet memory and the light of a bright example."

Stuck, who showed a sensitivity far beyond that of most of his Protestant colleagues, saw the heritage of Alaska disappearing. After his ascent of Denali, the original name for Mount McKinley, he commented:

When the inhabited wilderness has become an uninhabited wilderness, when the only people who will ever make their homes in it are exterminated, when the placer-gold is gone and the white men have gone also, when the last interior Alaskan town is like Diamond City and Glacier City and Bearpaw City and Roosevelt City; and Bettles and Rampart and Coldfoot; and Cleary City and Delta City and Vault City and a score of others; let at least the native names of these great mountains remain to show that there once dwelt in the land a simple, hardy race who braved successfully the rigors of its climate and inhospitality of their environment and flourished, until the septic contact of a superior race put corruption into their blood.

While the national park that surrounds it has been re-named Denali ("big one" or "high one"), the mountain itself continues to bear the name of the Republican twenty-fifth President of the United States.

The map of Alaska has been redrawn in such a way that its original inhabitants might be hard pressed to know its meaning. Stripped of their language, they could be lost in their own land—and many have been, many are.

It was not until 1924—the year Rasmussen met his last shaman—that Alaska Natives were granted citizenship. By then, most of their land was lost to them. In 1968, oil was discovered—an estimated 10 billion barrels—at Prudhoe Bay. In 1971, President Nixon, pressured by those looking toward the huge new discovery, signed the Alaska Native Claims Settlement Act. With that dramatic stroke, Alaska's 50,000 Natives were granted title to 44 million acres of land and given a cash settlement of $962.5 million. To administer the new wealth, a network of regional and village corporations was established. Eligible Natives—those with at least one-quarter Native blood and born before December 18, 1971—became shareholders in the various corporations. In exchange, the Trans-Alaska Pipeline could be built. With a signature, the Alaska Native had been made a member of a corporation in exchange for tribal lands. Natives born after the enrollment date did not qualify. Older Natives not included at that time for one reason or another—there were approximately two hundred—also did not qualify. The "left-outs" and the "New Natives" entered a political and personal limbo.

Alaska's black heart was now cracked open. The eight-hundred-mile pipeline to Valdez, constructed at a cost of $8 billion, went into production in 1977. The first tanker carrying North Slope crude pulled out of the Valdez terminal on August 2 of that year. In the beginning, about 2 million barrels of oil moved through the pipeline each day, at

5.5 miles per hour. The flow came to represent 25 percent of daily American production.

Now, with reserves dwindling, the hemorrhage slows. The state grows alarmed, and the cry goes up: Develop ANWR, the Arctic National Wildlife Refuge! The non-renewable resource is coming to an end, and Alaska, which depends on it for 85 percent of its income, faces serious consequences. But the oil companies move on to the Russian Far East, where oil can be extracted with far fewer environmental demands.

The North Slope Borough, which encompasses Barrow and the Arctic oil patch, threatens secession. The North Slope's future, however, is tentative and symbiotic. There has never been a treaty with the Inupiat Eskimos or with other indigenous peoples of Alaska, but they are locked into a system too complicated—and too costly—to undo. It is a delicate and dangerous dance, but a dance missing the shaman, missing the mask, missing the essential link with the world of spirit.

The battle cry of development versus nondevelopment intensifies as the separation between self and earth widens. Alaska Natives are shareholders now, their profits dependent on extraction of natural resources from the heart of their lands. But without the shaman, the people are cut off from their power. Their place has been transformed into corporate shares and the dividends those shares yield. It is not a place where their descendants can stand.

The pipeline runs eight hundred miles from Prudhoe Bay to Valdez, the ice-free port at the head of Prince William Sound. From there, on huge tankers, Alaska's black blood is shipped. It travels out into the Gulf of Alaska and down the coast by the huge glaciers surrounding Lituya Bay, weaving among icebergs. Kah Lituya never sleeps; his bear-slaves roll their heads to sniff the wind for unwelcome intruders.

The poems led me. Serving as writer-in-residence at the Alaska State Library, I traveled one year throughout the state, giving programs wherever they could be set up. Easter week I was in Kotzebue, just above the Arctic Circle. It was light from very early in the morning until late at night, but the temperature seldom rose above zero, and the Chukchi Sea was frozen as far as I could see. On Palm Sunday, I attended services at the Quaker church, where Eskimo women rose in their flowered "parkis" to ask forgiveness. One requested the hymn "His Eye Is on the Sparrow," and the congregation rose as a unit to sing.

CHAPTER V

Lady Franklin's Search: A Theory

I soon would leave the office and lose my last—my only—connection with Kent, and he was growing fainter as the days turned into weeks and the conversations about his possible whereabouts faltered. Already his voice was almost out of range, cracking and garbled. He had traveled to a place we could not reach. Much was flowing away.

Day after day for seven years I had faithfully walked or driven the very short distance from our house to this job, as editor of the state's conservation magazine and as supervisor of the public communications section. I held those two titles and juggled those two workloads.

The headquarters of the Department of Fish and Game is located in a mustard-yellow building that is a converted

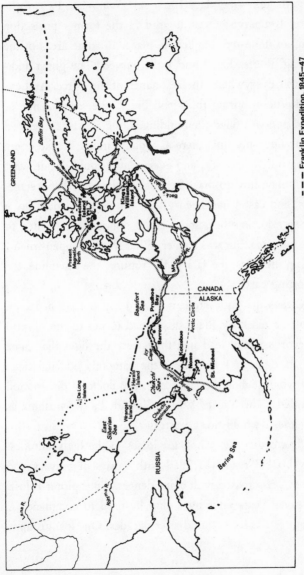

--- Franklin Expedition, 1845—47
.... Franklin Searches, 1847—59
-··-··- De Long's Jeannette Expedition, 1879—81
——— Bartlett's <u>Karluk</u> Expedition, 1913—14

movie theater—the place I first saw *Star Wars*. Part of the section I supervised was housed in the former projection room, an unheated, bunkerlike place. In some areas of the building, floors sloped and walls curved. The ghost audience was everywhere, the resonance of the Force. And every afternoon during the 3 P.M. break, the scent of microwaved popcorn filled the building. Long ago I had decided to look upon my time there as a daily drama, a soap opera lacking only a sponsor, and every day I could decide what role to play, how to make best use of the remarkable stage, props, and cast I had been given. But soon I would leave this stage for another, and I could not see it. I wanted to write full-time, but was I able? What would happen when I gave up the titles, the salary, the routine, the discipline, the supporting cast?

Always the good student—I did my honors paper on use of the mask by Fielding—I had to get to the library. The words would lead me; they were the light that came from the lantern I held over the camouflaged landscape. They would define the landscape. My doctoral dissertation was titled "The Tao of Writing." With Lady Sarashina as my guide, I would not go astray.

Thus began my search for losses in the high latitudes. Every book I read was filled with stories of bravery and egotism, crisscrossed with coincidences. An explorer is lost, then saved years later by a ship he used to command. A message in a cairn is found after decades. One lost group is saved by the cached stores of another. A ship changes name, occupation, location, floating through maritime history like a ghost, only to reappear at a critical moment; those lost and saved stumble upon one another in the Arctic wastes—or don't.

One day, out of this strange world of far-north connections missed and made fell a small book published by the Alaska Historical Society (and to my knowledge, nowhere else)—the journal of Sophia Cracroft, edited by historian Robert DeArmond, of Sitka. Sophia Cracroft was the niece of Sir John Franklin, and her book offered up Lady Jane Franklin's theory of disappearance: *The record—the written message—is everything. Press on until you have every bit of evidence that is possible. Never give up. Keep the search alive. While the search lives, the missing person lives. While the search continues, hope continues. As the record is put together, the monument to the missing person grows. If the record is substantial enough, the missing person cannot be lost, ever. Trust the written word.*

Lady Sarashina had guided me, as I knew she would. I filled with excitement. This small, strange book of a month-long visit to the nearby town of Sitka more than a hundred years before had been put there, published, just for me. I read it over and over. Dates and details of chronology and geography took on urgency. Perhaps I could chart Lady Franklin's search; perhaps I could give meaning to my own.

* * *

It was 1870, seven years before Sheldon Jackson arrived in nearby Wrangell to claim the Native soul and three years after the sale of Alaska to the United States, when Lady Jane Franklin sailed into Sitka. Her husband, Sir John Franklin, had left for the Arctic in 1845. Because of her efforts, a record finally was found stating that he had died in 1847 and verifying that he had indeed completed the Northwest Passage.

At age seventy-eight, Lady Franklin still had not given up. In Sitka, the former capital of Russian America, previously known as New Archangel, she hoped to find letters and documents from her husband's missing ships. She thought there was a chance such records might have filtered down to the capital and still be stored in some archive.

She arrived in Sitka on May 12 with her niece, Sophia Cracroft, who recorded the month-long visit. Two weeks after arriving, the two women discovered that letters they had been expecting from home had been sent on to Kodiak, far to the north, where they had originally planned to travel. Lady Franklin decided to travel after them. The ship, the *Constantine*, would go by way of Hinchinbrook Island, at the mouth of Prince William Sound.

Lady Franklin was anxious to go. The captain, however, citing possible bad weather, delays, and lack of insurance, refused. Wrangles over the cost of accommodations ensued, and rain set in. The two women came to see themselves as imprisoned. Miss Cracroft's journal ends abruptly on June 14: "Another lovely day, wh. gave us the opportunity of getting a view from the Govt. House—so we went up there at 12 and Genl. Tompkins came down from his office. We saw well out to sea but the view up the straits wh. on a clear day extends to 60 miles"

The search for Sir John Franklin, and the answers to the mysterious disappearance of his expedition, continue. It is a mystery that marks the end of the search for the Northwest Passage and opens the race for conquest of the North Pole. It is a mystery that even modern technology has failed fully to explain and that continues to be the subject of study and debate. I do not know when, if ever, Lady Franklin caught up with her letters. Words from her missing husband never caught up with her, but she continued to travel as long as her body would allow her. It is a story of still empty places on the map. It is a story of hope.

On August 16, 1826, Sir John Franklin, on his third Arctic expedition and second to the northernmost coastline of America, reached and named Prudhoe Bay, the source of Alaska's great oil reserves. The man whose name would become synonymous with Arctic tragedy had found the bay, the core of Alaska's now diminishing oilfields, but of course he did not know its pooled black secret.

Franklin was to have continued west to meet Lieutenant Beechey at Icy Cape, 160 miles away. Icy Cape, on the northwest coast of Alaska at latitude 70°29′ north, was the farthest point north that Captain James Cook had reached forty-eight years earlier. If Franklin had reached it, having come from the mouth of the Mackenzie River, the British would have virtually completed the Northwest Passage. The fog, ice, and wind, however, were too much. Franklin decided that the season had turned and it was pointless to go forward. His previous experience on the ice-lashed coast had given him sufficient lessons. Once more winter had closed in on the polar regions.

Our first view of what was to become Alaska's tenuous economic lifeline was not encouraging, as Franklin gives it to us:

> Between Point Anxiety and Point Chandos, which is eight miles further to the westward, the land was occasionally seen; but after rounding the latter point we lost sight of it, and steered to the westward across the mouth of Yarborough Inlet, the soundings varying from five feet to two fathoms. . . . A temporary dispersion of the fog showed that we were surrounded with banks nearly on a level with the water, and protected to seaward by a large body of ice lying aground. The patch of gravel on which we were encamped, was about five hundred yards in circumference, destitute of water, and

with no more drift wood than a few willow branches, sufficient to make one fire.

Concerned only with the weather, and mindful of his past experiences, he made the decision to turn back. The rendezvous with Beechey, only 160 miles away, did not occur.

From that third expedition, Franklin went on to govern prisoners in Van Diemen's Land (Tasmania) until he was chosen by the British Admiralty to complete exploration of the Northwest Passage. In 1845, at age fifty-nine, he returned to the Arctic. His disappearance challenged the entire Victorian view of the Arctic and triggered the largest search and the most concentrated exploration the world had known. He was lost with 128 men and two ships, the *Terror* and the *Erebus*, in an area so huge and little known that ten years passed before conclusive evidence could be brought out that all on the expedition had perished. Franklin and his men were last seen by a whaler on July 26, 1845, anchored to an iceberg in Lancaster Sound, leading out of Baffin Bay. The season to traverse the Northwest Passage had not yet arrived. For Franklin it would come, bringing ultimate success, but with fatal results.

The British government posted a ten-thousand-pound reward for information about the missing expedition. Early in 1848 the search began. Over the next twelve years, fifty parties set out in the quest. Huge sums were expended. Lady Jane Franklin financed five wholly or in part. The search was three-pronged: from the northwest coast of what is now Alaska; from the mouth of the Mackenzie; and from the east. The interweavings and cross-references of the men and ships that searched during that decade have reverberated across Alaska for generations and are woven indelibly into its history. The western thrust, especially, provided a contact with indigenous peoples that had a lasting effect. To the present day, the search continues—not now for emotional but purely for academic reasons. Relics occasionally turn up. New technologies are applied, new questions raised.

As the Franklin searchers spread out over the frozen, wind-carved spaces of the Arctic, they looked not only for ships and men but for cairns, rock piles in which explorers placed records of their journeys. Here in these cairns—or buried ten feet true north of them, to protect the contents from intruders—might be found information critical to the search: projected route and condition of the party, as well as previous routes, discoveries, accomplishments, and problems. This was the flight plan, the press release, the health report, the newspaper, the broadcast, the mail delivery system of Arctic exploration. Though random, it was critical, sometimes meaning the difference between a lost party's being found and saved or not. It could also mean the difference between a territorial claim being held valid or not. An extraordinary example is that of the 1884 rescue of Lieutenant Adolphus W. Greely at Cape Sabine, Ellesmere Island, after his failed attempt at the pole. The contents of two cairns brought his rescuers to him and six of his men at the point of death. They were the only survivors of the twenty-five-man Lady Franklin Bay Expedition, which had set out three years before.

In 1848, Franklin searchers Captain Thomas Moore of the *Plover*, Captain Henry Kellett of the *Herald*, and Robert Sheldon of the *Nancy Dawson* entered Bering Strait at the start of the western thrust. Already Sir John Richardson and Dr. John Rae had canoed up the Mackenzie and started exploring east along the coast, while Captain Sir James Clark Ross of the *Enterprise* and Captain E. J. Bird of the *Investigator* were traveling into Lancaster Sound, where Franklin had last been seen waiting for the ice to clear.

With Sir James Clark Ross was Francis Leopold Mc-Clintock, a young lieutenant who would join the Belcher expedition of 1852–54 and then lead Lady Jane Franklin's expedition on the *Fox*, 1857–59. McClintock was to master Arctic sledging, a skill that enabled him not only to succeed but also to open up new possibilities for travel in the high latitudes.

In 1850, ten ships assembled at Beechey Island, where Lancaster Sound gives way to Barrow Strait in what is now known as the District of Franklin, Northwest Territories. Three graves of men from the *Erebus* and *Terror* who had died during the first winter were found there, but no records in cairns to tell how they had died or which way the ships had headed or with what plans. There were no clues. The map was blank.

As expeditions set out, winter quickly returned to the Arctic to meet them. The searchers now were likely to become the searched. One significant case was that of Lieutenant Robert McClure and the *Investigator*, one of six search parties to leave England in 1850, and one that traveled from the west, Alaska. Held by the ice, he was finally rescued in 1853 in Bay of God's Mercy by Kellett, this time in command of the *Resolute*. The rescue came about, in no small measure, because McClure had strategically placed a message at Winter Harbour on Melville Island that Kellett's party found. Kellett ordered all hands off the ice-bound *Investigator* onto the *Resolute*, now locked herself in the ice of Melville Sound. Before the rescue, however, two of McClure's men sledged to Beechey Island; their trek, in technical terms, was considered completion of the Northwest Passage. Though claims were numerous and conflicting, the government awarded McClure the ten-thousand-pound prize for its discovery.

It was John Rae of the Hudson's Bay Company who found the first evidence of Franklin other than the three wordless graves on Beechey Island. Rae came across an Eskimo who told him that a large party of white men had died of starvation a long distance to the west and beyond a large river (Back's or Fish River). The Eskimos had found about thirty-five bodies. Their condition and what was found in their kettles gave evidence of cannibalism. The Eskimos provided relics—pieces of watches and compasses, silver forks and spoons, and a small plate engraved "Sir John Franklin, K.C.B."

Rae received the government's ten-thousand-pound reward for information on Franklin. Another Hudson's Bay employee provided more relics. The Admiralty closed the case. The Crimean War took center stage, and the search for the Northwest Passage was considered accomplished. There were other boundaries to be pushed.

But the British public would not accept a tale of cannibalism, and Lady Jane Franklin would not give up hope. She petitioned the government to go on with the search. In 1856, she wrote to Viscount Palmerston:

> I have cherished the hope, in common with others, that we are not waiting in vain. Should, however, that decision unfortunately throw upon me the responsibility and the cost of sending out a vessel myself, I beg to assure your Lordship that I shall not shrink, either from that weighty responsibility, or from the sacrifice of my entire available fortune for the purpose, supported as I am in my convictions by such high authorities as those whose opinions are on record in your Lordship's hands, and by the hearty sympathy of many more.

But before I take upon myself so heavy an obligation, it is my bounden duty to entreat Her Majesty's Government not to disregard the arguments which have led so many competent and honorable men to feel that our country's honor is not satisfied, whilst a mystery which has excited the sympathy of the civilized world, remains uncleared. Nor less would I entreat you to consider what must be the unsatisfactory consequences, if any endeavors should be made to quench all further efforts for this object. . . .

Surely, then, I may plead for such men, that a careful search be made for any possible survivor, that the bones of the dead be sought for and gathered together, that their buried records be unearthed, or recovered from the hands of the Esquimaux, and above all, that their last written words, so precious to their bereaved families and friends, be saved from destruction. . . .

This final and exhausting search is all I seek in behalf of the first and only martyrs to Arctic discovery in modern times, and it is all I ever intend to ask.

Lady Franklin now requested a ship. Extraordinarily, it was the *Resolute*, Kellett's search ship, which had rescued McClure and which had been, herself, abandoned in the ice. An American whaler had found her floating in Davis Strait, a thousand miles to the east of her ice prison. Through Lady Franklin's efforts, the United States Congress purchased her for forty thousand dollars and presented her to

Great Britain. The request for recommissioning what Lady Franklin took to be a consecrated ship was denied, however. Another way must be found, another ship. Determined to go on, she then raised funds for her fifth private expedition. She outfitted the *Fox,* a small, 177-ton yacht, and put McClintock in charge. She also told McClintock where to search: Go south, she said, south of Lancaster Sound. She knew her husband's orders and that he would have followed them. Far too much time and human life had been wasted in the north.

Lady Franklin and her constant companion, Sophia Cracroft, saw the *Fox* off. Under way in the Atlantic, McClintock opened and read his instructions, which Lady Franklin had unwillingly set down. They asked, of course, that rescue of any survivors be the chief goal: "To this object I wish every other to be subordinate; and next to it in importance is the recovery of the unspeakably precious documents of the expedition, public and private, and the personal relics of my dear husband and his companions." The third goal was confirmation of success in crossing the Northwest Passage.

From 1857 to 1859, McClintock rigorously pursued the threefold search and directions Lady Franklin had set. He headed first for King William Island. On the Boothia Peninsula coast, he encountered an Inuit wearing a naval button on his coat. The Eskimo told a story similar to that which Rae had been told. McClintock offered to buy any relics. A large number were provided: more buttons, knives, ship's wood. Later McClintock met the band of Inuits again, with a young man in their company who told of two ships, one of which had sunk off King William Land, the other of which had broken up on shore. McClintock obtained more relics, more descriptions. Soon he came across his first Franklin skeleton. He looked for any records of the expedition claiming discovery of the Northwest Passage, but there were none. Empty cairns indicated that the Eskimos too had followed the course of the tragedy.

But finally came the breakthrough. It was Lieutenant Hobson, who had served on the *Plover* and who was second in command, who found the document, in a cairn at Point Victory, on the northwest coast of King William Land. This cairn had been built by James Clark Ross in 1831, on his voyage of discovery of the magnetic North Pole.

When McClintock got there, he was shocked. Strewn about the cairn was a four-foot-high pile of clothing and articles, much of it absurdly unnecessary to survival.

As McClintock tells the story,

That record is indeed a sad and touching relic of our lost friends, and, to simplify its contents, I will point out separately the double story it so briefly tells. In the first place, the record paper was one of the printed forms usually supplied to discovery ships for the purpose of being enclosed in bottles and thrown overboard at sea, in order to ascertain the set of the currents, blanks being left for the date and position; any person finding one of these records is requested to forward it to the Secretary of the Admiralty, with a note of time and place; and this request is printed upon it in six different languages. Upon it was written, apparently by Lieutenant Gore, as follows:

Lt. Graham Gore, survivor of the *Terror's* 1837 expedition with George Back.

28 of May 1847	H.M. ships *Erebus* and *Terror* wintered in the ice in lat. 70°05′ N.; long. 98°23′ W.

Having wintered in 1846–47 at Beechey Island, in lat. 74°43′28″ N., long. 91°39′15″ W., after having ascended Wellington Channel to lat. 77°, and returned by the west side of Cornwallis Island.

Sir John Franklin commanding the expedition.
All well.
Party consisting of 2 officers and 6 men left the ships on Monday 24th May, 1847.

GM. Gore, Lieut.
Chas. F. Des Voeux, Mate

McClintock states that the wintering dates should read "1845–46" and applauds the success of the expedition to this point. Dramatically, he continues: "But alas! round the margin of the paper upon which Lieutenant Gore in 1847 wrote those words of hope and promise, another hand had subsequently written the following words":

April 25, 1848. —H.M. ships *Terror* and *Erebus* were deserted on the 22nd April, 5 leagues N.N.W. of this, having been beset since 12th September, 1846. The officers and crews, consisting of 105 souls, under the command of Capt. F.R.M. Crozier, landed here in lat. 69°37', 42", long. 98°41' W. [This] paper was found by Lt. Irving under the cairn supposed to have been built by Sir James Ross in 1831—where it had been deposited (4 miles to the northward)—by the late Commander Gore in June 1847. Sir James Ross' pillar has not however been found and the paper has been transferred to this position which is that in which Sir J Ross pillar was erected— Sir John Franklin died on the 11th June 1847; and the total loss by deaths in the expedition has been to this date 9 officers and 15 men.

The addendum was signed by Crozier, captain of the *Terror*, and James Fitzjames, captain of the *Erebus*. By his name, Crozier noted, "and start (on) to-morrow, 26th, for Back's Fish River."

Continuing with the search, McClintock found the ship's longboat on a sledge with the two skeletons Hobson had come across earlier. Again, a large number of relics lay about, including books, clothing, watches, shotguns, and toilet articles. Tea and forty pounds of chocolate were the only food found. McClintock returned to England with a long list of relics:

> A 6-inch dip circle by Robinson, marked I 22. A case of medicines, consisting of 25 small bottles, canister of pills, ointment, plaster, oiled silk, etc. A 2-foot rule, two joints of the cleaning rod of a gun, and two small copper spindles, probably for dog-vanes of boats. The circular brass plate broken out of a wooden gun-case, and engraved "C. H. Osmer, R.N." The field glass and German silver top of a 2-foot telescope, a coffee canister, a piece of a brass curtain rod. The record tin and the record, dated 25th of April, 1848. A 6-inch double frame sextant, on which the owner's name is engraved, "Frederick Hornby, R.N."

The ships, according to McClintock, had perished within sight of the headlands Ross had named Cape Franklin and Cape Jane Franklin eighteen years before, but the good news he brought was that the Franklin party had achieved "virtual completion of the Northwest Passage." From then on, members of the expedition were hailed as "martyrs" of the quest.

Lady Franklin had achieved success, if only partial. Her expedition, following her explicit orders, had found the only record of the lost expedition ever to be found, to this day. It was enough to prove her husband's expedition successful. It was enough to give her husband—whatever his true level of accomplishments and abilities—lasting fame as the greatest explorer of the Arctic.

But the search for Franklin was far from complete and continues today, a crowded map of unanswered questions.

During the years from 1864 to 1869, the American newspaper entrepreneur Charles Francis Hall collected stories, found some bodies (one of which he brought to the United States) and some relics. He was told by Inuits that papers from the expedition had been given to children to play with, "and after a while all of it (a book) got torn to pieces. He says if any one goes there in summer he may find pieces of paper about there." He was also given more testimony as to cannibalism. (He himself met a grisly fate on his next expedition—to the North Pole: He was poisoned on board, apparently by the doctor who headed his scientific team.)

From 1878 to 1880, U.S. Army Lieutenant Frederick Schwatka, who would also become associated with a newspaper's push for fame in the north, became the last to interview Inuit observers of the Franklin expedition. He too was told that documents from the Franklin expedition had been given to children. There could be no further hope that such papers would be found or that there would ever be conclusive evidence as to the fate of the party.

The annotated record found by Hobson and McClintock stood with its sad rubrics as a final goodbye. The precious last words for which Lady Franklin so ardently hoped had been committed to the elements.

In 1926, Peter Norberg found a skull on the Adelaide Peninsula which analysis indicated came from the Franklin expedition. In 1936, the remains of three other expedition members were found nearby.

In 1967, Project Franklin was carried out by the Canadian Armed Forces in honor of the centennial of Canada's confederation. During the project, fifty-two men from the different military units sought relics and further information from most of the known relevant sites. Divers searched near O'Reilly Island, where Inuit testimony indicates one of the ships sank. Nothing was found underwater, but pieces of equipment were located on the northern beaches of the island.

In 1981 and 1982, Dr. Owen Beattie, a forensic anthropologist, examined bones from King William Land. In 1984 he exhumed and examined the body of John Torrington from his Beechey Island grave, and in 1986 the bodies of the two other crewmen buried there, John Hartnell and William Braine. Although Beattie found high levels of lead and lead poisoning from poorly soldered tin cans, which undoubtedly contributed to the collapse of the party, lead does not provide the entire answer, any more than scurvy does. Franklin's skeleton has never been found; he might well have been buried at sea.

Theories abound and searches continue. But it was a group of Eskimo children, undoubtedly, who held in their hands and committed to the winds the final record of what had truly happened. What, finally, sets a person free? To hold last written words?

I have not yet been able to throw out my father's letters, though he is dead ten years and estranged for many more before that. I carried them all the way from Colorado to Alaska, this land of last hope. They grow damp and fragile in my basement. Still, I can't throw them out, knowing full well they do not give answers. Knowing the pain they keep alive. Feeding my sadness and dismay. After all those silent years, my father disinherited me. In his last will and testament, I do not exist.

While Martin was greeting us at the ferry in the dark of that October morning when we first arrived in Juneau, someone backed into his Volkswagen, crushing the driver's door. Reunited, we drove in tandem through the quiet streets of our new city—a place that can be reached only by water or by air. The house he led us to was painted green. A flowerbed running between one wall and the sidewalk overflowed with nasturtiums: a lasting memory of yellow and orange in the first light of that first northern dawn.

CHAPTER VI

Lieutenant De Long: Proof

Lady Franklin was right in one regard. A powerful written record can keep a lost person alive. One such record—and one Lady Franklin would have exulted in—was that of George Washington De Long's *Jeannette* expedition to the North Pole. Edited and promoted by his widow, Emma, De Long's journal indeed seems proof of Lady Franklin's burning theorem. I read it with mounting excitement; the path of words continued to open before me.

Significantly, the first major American attempt on the pole was bankrolled and pushed by the newspaper baron James Gordon Bennett, publisher and owner of the *New York Herald*, a man known as much for his flamboyant personal life as for his journalistic career. Bennett was anxious for a scoop to follow that of his reporter Henry Stanley in locating the African missionary Dr. Livingstone. He thought the North Pole was a good place to find it.

In 1877, Bennett purchased the steam yacht *Pandora*, formerly owned by Sir Allen Young, who had tried to sail the Northwest Passage with her in 1875–76. Earlier, in 1857, Young had accompanied Leopold McClintock and Lieutenant Hobson as volunteer officers on board Lady Jane Franklin's yacht *Fox* in the successful search for news of the Franklin expedition. Young served McClintock as sailing master, contributing, as McClintock notes, "not only his valuable services but largely of his private funds to the expedition." When the three officers split into separate search parties, Young explored Prince of Wales Island, adding significant geographical information, though he discovered no news of Franklin.

Young's former yacht was refitted and renamed *Jeannette*. Bennett put U.S. Navy Lieutenant George Washington De Long in command of the expedition, which departed from San Francisco on July 8, 1879, with thirty-three on board. Its destination was the pole, by way of Wrangel Island, north of Siberia between the Chukchi and East Siberian seas. For more than two years there was silence; the fate of the party was unknown. Bennett was to get more than he had bargained for.

On December 21, 1881, the U.S. Navy received a telegram, the message of which had originated in Irkutsk, Siberia, announcing that the *Jeannette* had been crushed in the ice on June 11, 1881, at latitude 77°15' north, longitude 157° east. (It was the same day that Sir John Franklin had died on the other side of the Arctic in 1847.) Thirteen men of the *Jeannette* had survived, not including De Long. The struggles of those men rank among the most harrowing stories of Arctic tragedy, and the story of those who found them speaks to the incredible lengths that human endurance, and loyalty, can be pushed.

It was a story, like so many Arctic stories, that began and ended with hope and that fed itself along its brutal way on tender moments of compassion. Like many explorers before him and after him, De Long looked especially to birds as messengers. Early in the journal account (which we have by such miracle), he comments:

> When off the coast of Brazil, and a hundred miles from any land, two little birds flew on board the ship to rest; one was a tomtit and the other a field lark. They had evidently been blown off shore by a gale of wind. They showed no fear but refused to eat anything, though everything in the shape of grain which the ship contained was offered to them, and even some lively cheese, which might be a special inducement to insectivorous birds. They would take no nourishment at all, and the tomtit died of hunger and exhaustion. The steward, a Swiss, composed some verses upon his melancholy fate, and these, with the latitude and longitude, were put with the little

tomtit into a bottle, which was addressed inside to the "Herald" and thrown over board. It has not yet reached its destination. The field lark flew out of the cabin door, left open by accident, and could not be recovered. It flew off the ship and then made successive efforts to return, but its strength gave out and it sank at last into the water.

De Long was convinced that the pole could be reached by Wrangel Land, which he took to be a landmass, not an island. The Japan current, he hoped, would open a way and allow him to travel up the coast of Wrangel Land, leaving records in cairns every twenty-five miles, with only a final dash over the ice to the pole necessary to complete his mission. It was a novel approach, as was that of using hot-air balloons, a concept he and Bennett seriously contemplated and then rejected—a concept that was not tried until 1897, when the Swedish scientist Andrée set out for the pole in the *Eagle*.

After a stop at St. Michael's, Alaska, to take on dogs, sledges, and fur clothing, the *Jeannette* moved north until caught by the icepack near Herald Island, the island named by Kellett and Moore during their search for Franklin in the western Arctic (and, strangely, repeating the name of Bennett's newspaper, the paper looking for a scoop). The *Jeannette* began an inexorable drift. As the crew passed Wrangel Land, they discovered, too late, that it is a small island and not a landmass.

As De Long states early in his detailed journal, "This is a glorious country to learn patience in." There was no return for the *Jeannette*. By the summer of 1880, De Long's outlook had grown morose. There was illness, including insanity, among the crew; a constant consumption of food and fuel; and the endless drift, which took them everywhere but where they wanted to go. Boredom settled hard upon them, though a rigorous discipline was maintained. In keeping both a personal journal and a log (until the ship was abandoned and he kept only one account), De Long made a meticulous record of the disintegration of a dream.

June 21 [1880]: . . . Observations show us that we have drifted, since the 19th, eleven and three tenths miles to S. 68 degrees E. Discouraging, very. And yet my motto is, "Hope on, hope ever." A very good one it is when one's surroundings are more natural than ours; but situated as we are it is better in the abstract than in realization. There can be no greater wear and tear on a man's mind and patience than this life in the pack. The absolute monotony; the unchanging round of hours; the awakening to the same things and the same conditions that one saw just before losing one's self in sleep; the same faces; the same dogs; the same ice; the same conviction that to morrow will be exactly the same as to-day, if not more disagreeable; the absolute impotence to do anything, to go anywhere, or to change one's situation an iota; the realization that food is being consumed and fuel burned with no valuable result, beyond sustaining life; the knowledge that nothing has been accomplished thus far to save this expedition from being denominated an utter failure; all these things crowd in with irresistible force on my reasoning powers each night as I sit down to reflect upon the events of the day, and but for some still small voice within me that tells me this can hardly be the ending of all my labor and zeal, I should be tempted to despair.

All our books are read, our stories related; our games of chess, cards, and checkers long since discontinued. When we assemble in the morning at breakfast we make daily a fresh start. Any dreams, amusing or peculiar, are related and laughed over. Theories as to whether we shall eventually drift N.E. or N.W. are brought forward and discussed. . . .

One dream stood out as significant. On October 30, 1879, the ship's doctor related a dream of the previous night in which he accompanied the survivors of Sir John Franklin's last expedition on their journey to the Great Fish River. In the dream, he suddenly was back in the cabin of the *Jeannette*, explaining to Franklin some of their new equipment, such as Edison's electric machine, the anemometer, and the telephone. Franklin, after listening to the explanations and viewing the articles, tersely remarked, "Your electric machine is not worth a damn, and your anemometer is just the same." Only the telephone won his approval.

According to Chinese divination, it was the worst possible kind of dream. Dreaming of one's own setting means that one's ch'i, or energy, is oppressed and cannot escape; it has nowhere to go.

It was exactly two years later, to the day, that De Long, dying of starvation on the Lena River delta, wrote his last journal entry, one of those final journal entries of the north ending with no punctuation.

The log also recounts moments of saving grace: the Chinese cooks, Ah Sam and Charles Tong Sing, flying kites on the ice alongside the stricken ship; wild chases after polar bears; the antics of the dogs; the discovery of mosquitoes and the sighting of rainbows and of the exquisite Ross's gull, of meteors and northern lights and halos with prismatic colors around the moon; a view of the snowy spars against a moonlit sky. There were breakthroughs of ingenuity: the use of seal and walrus blubber for fuel and a windmill to run a pipe. There was the assurance of kindness: The sick were treated with infinite patience and compassion.

But always there was the imprisonment and the silence and the maddening observations. They were always on the move but going nowhere, "like a modern *Flying Dutchman.*"

In May and June of 1881 the crew sighted, tracked, named, and claimed Jeannette and Henrietta islands. A landing was made on Henrietta Island on June 3. The only

had been swallowed.

On their way, they discovered and claimed Bennett Island, leaving a record at Cape Emma. The party of thirty-three was still intact. On September 5, on Kotelnoi Island, near some huts, they discovered various artifacts, including a coin with the date 1840. The party was still intact.

On September 12, a gale separated the three boats. De Long and his group struggled on, reaching the Lena River delta. They saw nothing more of the other two boats. One disappeared, never to be seen again. The third made landfall, but the surviving crews never reunited.

Starting their agonizing voyage inland in search of a settlement, De Long and his men struggled to maintain discipline and momentum. As travel became more difficult, they jettisoned sleeping bags, one of the two tents, and other equipment. There were signs of human life, and even of civilization, which encouraged them. At one point they came to a hut with, among other things, the remains of a checkerboard. There continued to be hope—sometimes deer tracks, once the print of a moccasin in snow, fox traps, some wooden plates and forks.

A month from the end, there was still hope: "September 29: . . . I caused this morning a black flag to be displayed on poles lashed together, about twenty feet in height, but the weather is so thick I do not think it will attract anybody. A large gull was drawn toward it, and Alexey shot him, ensuring us gull soup for supper."

Although some game was secured—sometimes deer, sometimes gull or ptarmigan—the food supply ran out, and the last dog was shot and eaten. Soon alcohol was all that was left; and that was carefully rationed out, served with hot water. It helped to stave off hunger pangs. Two members of the party had been sent on ahead, but it was too late. With one man unable to walk and the entire group growing weaker and more disabled, De Long's motto ran out. *Jeannette/Pandora*'s hope, that cruelly seductive siren song, was silenced. Keeping his journal to the very end, the fastidious commander entered the names of the dead and the dying, breaking off, finally, with no punctuation, just as Sophia Cracroft's journal of the visit to Sitka ends. The last entry is dated October 30, 1881: "140th day—Boyd & Gertz died during night—Mr. Collins dying"

The crew of the second boat to reach land got to a settlement and found help. When the two members of the De Long crew reached another settlement, however, they could not make themselves understood. The Russian natives, not knowing what the desperate men wanted, sent them south to their shipmates, of whom they had knowledge. By then winter had set in, making further travel impossible. There could be no help for De Long. In all, twenty of the original thirty-three died, including De Long.

On March 23 of the next year, Melville, one of the group who had landed in the second boat and reached a settlement, found the bodies of the De Long party. He found De Long with his left arm raised above the snow. In Melville's words: "I found the ice journal about three or four feet in the rear of De Long; that is, it looked as though he had been lying down, and with his left hand tossed the book over his shoulder to the rear, or the eastward of him."

De Long had been trying, apparently, with his last action, to throw the journal to higher ground, where it would not be claimed by the inevitable spring floods. That he was successful—that it was found and that it has come to us intact—is just the miracle for which Lady Franklin so urgently hoped and in which she placed such faith.

During the summer of 1882, searches were made of the delta for members of the third boat, which had disappeared in the gale of September 12. Nothing was found. The secretary of the Navy gave instructions, however, to bring back the remains of De Long and his group. Twenty-five thousand dollars was appropriated. In the spring of 1883, the bodies were removed from their icy vault on the Lena delta. De Long's body was returned to New York for a hero's burial.

In 1884, three years after the *Jeannette* went under the ice, relics were picked up from an ice floe on the southwest coast of Greenland. Based on that evidence of circumpolar drift, Fridtjof Nansen set out in 1893 in his custom-built *Fram*, which succeeded in drifting around the pole in similar clockwise fashion, also in three years. And in 1903 Roald Amundsen, having learned from the *Jeannette* and the *Fram*, set sail in the tiny forty-seven-ton *Gjoa* on what would become a successful—and again three-year—east-to-west crossing of the Northwest Passage.

De Long lived on.

I took Helen to enroll in our neighborhood school, Harborview, just a few blocks away. Helen, just starting first grade, was assigned to Mrs. Bibb. I wondered who this Mrs. Bibb might be, that she would take my daughter, my firstborn. Suspicious, I looked at her there across a roomful of children: Mary Ellen. She was pregnant. I learned later that she had five more at home, a huge log house that her husband, Pete, had built at the end of the Thane Road, where the pavement south ends. A dedicated teacher who took to heart the needs of each of her students, she became my dear friend, my compass. I loved her. Some years later, when she died suddenly and unnecessarily—the result of medical negligence—while away in Montana for the summer, I felt as if the world had fallen away beneath me.

CHAPTER VII
Captain Bartlett:
Proof and Other Stories

Bob Bartlett, captain of the *Karluk*, a ship pulled by the powers of Arctic exploration and current in the same direction and into the same fate as the *Jeannette*, had no wife waiting at home.

The story of the *Karluk*, commanded by the egotistical explorer Vilhjalmur Stefansson, rivaled the *Jeannette* in tragedy, and overshadowed what otherwise was an expedition of great significance. It was a tragedy well documented, one that spared little of the long, harrowing—and unnecessary—escapade. And it was a conscious tragedy, for its participants had De Long's journal on board and followed it word by word, page by inexorable page, as if their destiny had been set forth. They also surmised that the *Karluk*'s fate would happen faster; the ship, though similar to the *Jeannette*, was not as sturdy.

Karluk means "fish" in Aleut. She was a 247-ton brigantine built in Oregon as a salmon tender for the Aleutian Islands fishery. Although she had been reinforced as a whaler and spent years in that industry until its decline, she was not built for ice. Stefansson, however, had traveled on her along the Alaskan coast during his expeditions of 1906–7 and 1908–12 and thought well of her.

The expedition Stefansson now undertook was the Arctic Expedition of 1913–18, which was to map the Beaufort Sea, the last great gap in the north polar map, and to study the Inuit along the way. Although he accomplished much of what he set out to do, discovering new islands and wresting much information from previously unknown areas, his expedition was to turn out very differently from what he had expected and cast a lifelong shadow over his career. One factor was his fault: The *Karluk* was not the ship for the job, and its crew was not properly prepared for what they were to face. Another factor was beyond his control: The winter of 1913–14 was one of unprecedented severity and duration. The combination of obstinacy and weather proved tragic.

In September, east of Barrow and not far from Prudhoe Bay, where Sir John Franklin turned back in 1826, the *Karluk* stuck fast in ice. Stefansson left her and her crew to go on by foot and hunt. He expected to be gone ten days, but as he watched, the *Karluk* began her fatal drift to the north and west, around the blank face of the polar clock, and he never saw her again. For five years he continued his part of the expedition to the east, aided by two small ships, the *Alaska* and the *Mary Sachs*.

Soon after Stefansson last looked on her, the *Karluk* vanished. There were no reported sightings as she was carried away to the fate of the *Jeannette*.

On board the drifting ship was an unusual assortment: twenty white men, including Robert A. Bartlett, the New-foundland-born American captain, who was to prove a re-markable leader and become a legend of Arctic exploration; an Inupiat family, consisting of Kuraluk, the father, Kiruk, the mother, and two young daughters, Helen and Mugpi, and a young Inupiat widower by the name of Kataktovik, all of whom contributed indispensably to the salvation of those who survived; sixteen dogs, and Nigeraurak, "Little Black One," the ship's cat, taken aboard by one of the crew in Victoria. (A bronze plaque commemorating the north-bound visit of the *Karluk* in 1913 is fixed to the waterfront wall across the street from the Empress Hotel in Victoria.)

As the *Karluk* drifted ever farther to the west and into the Arctic night, those aboard became ever more conscious that they were on the same fatal course followed by De Long and the *Jeannette* in 1879. Indeed, De Long's chart and the eight-hundred-page record of his journey, on board, were subjects of intense interest and scrutiny, and a constant comparison was maintained by the imprisoned crew. There was a difference, however: The *Jeannette* had drifted for nineteen months before being crushed, and the specially built *Fram*, following in her wake, had survived three years in the pack ice; it seemed unlikely that the insubstantial *Karluk*, a little fish tender, could hold up anywhere near as long as the *Jeannette*.

Christmas passed, with athletic events, a feast, and toasts to those at home. The cracking of the ice was growing louder, closer, sending shudders through the ship. The ice prisoners hurried with their preparations for what lay ahead after the *Karluk*. The sewing of skin clothes was particularly important. Captain Bartlett, with good nature, presided over the men at their needles; it was unusual work for the adventurers, but as the seasoned captain well knew, critical.

On January 10, 1914, ice gashed the *Karluk*'s side and water poured in. Captain Bartlett gave the order to abandon ship. Calmly the crew carried off all necessary stores and equipment and made ready the box houses that they had already built on the ice floe. Shortly after midnight the ship's flag was flown. Captain Bartlett, alone on board, played the full collection of records on the gramophone, one by one, throwing them into the galley stove's fire as they finished. He held out Chopin's "Funeral March." At 3:15 in the afternoon the *Karluk* settled down, the deck sinking under water. Captain Bartlett put the "Funeral

March" on the gramophone, then stepped off onto the ice and stood by as his ship disappeared into the blackness of the Arctic waters, the Canadian blue ensign fluttering. Seldom has a sinking ship experienced such a refined interment.

During his remarkable life, Bartlett was shipwrecked twelve times. Among many exploits, he captained the *Roosevelt*, Robert E. Peary's ship, and assisted Peary in becoming the first to attain the North Pole, in 1909. On that trip he was in command of the last group of supporters to turn back before Peary made his historic dash to the pole with Matthew Henson, four Eskimos, and forty dogs. At that point, where he turned back with the support group, Bartlett was a hundred miles farther north than anyone had been.

The stranded crew of *Karluk* settled into "Shipwreck Camp" on their ice floe three hundred miles off the northeast Siberian coast and eighty miles north of Wrangel Island. They listened in the darkness to the sickening roar of the moving ice. They were sufficiently supplied and as comfortable as could be expected, but clearly they had to take action. Captain Bartlett organized parties to cache supplies in a forward movement toward Wrangel Island. One group, led by the mate, Alexander "Sandy" Anderson, never reappeared. As crew member William Laird McKinlay said of them later, "They were never seen again, four young men with no grand ideas about exploring the Arctic, or finding new land, just four sailors trying to follow orders. Sandy Anderson was not yet twenty-one." Another group of four, led by the ship's doctor, chose to leave and break off on their own. They too were never seen again.

The survivors now left Shipwreck Camp, heading for Wrangel Island over what was to prove a torturous route of moving pack ice, which sometimes heaved huge ridges in front of them. They reached the frozen island on March 12, 1914.

Captain Bartlett, knowing it was essential to find help, struck out for the Siberian mainland with Kataktovik, the young Inupiat widower, leaving the rest of the party on Wrangel Island. He hoped to meet them with a ship in mid-July.

Experiencing extraordinary difficulties but moving with equally extraordinary speed, the two men traversed two hundred miles of pack ice to reach Siberia and then traveled seven hundred miles down the coast of the Chukchi Peninsula looking for a ship to Alaska. The trip took them fifty-four days.

During their first encounter with the Chukchis, they were asked, in sign language, if they had seen any sign of two hunters who had disappeared on the ice two years before. Further on, at Cape North (first seen and named by Captain Cook in 1778, as he turned south for Hawaii), they met a Native who claimed he had whaled on the *Karluk*. Continuing east and south down the peninsula, they came to a Native house at Cape Wankarem where they were entertained by records of Caruso and John McCormack, just as Rasmussen, to his consternation, was entertained ten years later in Arctic Canada by the shaman Igjugarjuk.

Traveling on, the two men encountered four Russian prospectors on their way to Cape North, near which were gold mines. The prospectors treated them generously, sharing their food. One spoke a little English. Bartlett wrote down his name on a slip of paper but lost it.

Kataktovik stayed at East Cape, waiting for a ship to take him across Bering Strait to Point Hope; he had joined the expedition at Point Barrow. At Emma Harbor, Bartlett managed to board the whaler *Herman,* which got him to St. Michael's on the Alaska coast. (St. Michael's was the final point of departure for the *Jeannette* in 1879.) There he found a telegraph and could finally alert the world to the plight of his crew back on Wrangel Island. The U.S. marshal at St. Michael's was a friend. In 1896 he had sailed into the Labrador fishing station where Bartlett was spending the summer; his ship was the *Hope.*

The United States revenue cutter *Bear* promised to help, as did the little schooner *King & Winge,* a halibut boat turned walrus hunter on her maiden voyage. On July 13, 1913, the *Bear*—angel and workhorse of the Arctic waters —had given *Karluk* a farewell salute in Nome as she headed north to her fate. Now, because of bad weather and other problems, the *Bear* was delayed, and *King & Winge* got to Wrangel Island first, on September 7, 1914. The party was later transferred to the *Bear.*

The rescue came just in time. Three men had died on the island, one of them—Breddy—by apparent suicide. By the next day, one of the two groups would have moved to another part of the island, making their rescue improbable. The death toll stood at eleven of the original twenty white men. The Inupiats all survived. It was their skill and courage that made life for others possible.

Later, writing his autobiography, Bartlett credited Kiruk (whom he refers to as Inaloo) with saving his feet, and thus his life. As the *Karluk* was sinking, Kiruk dashed into the captain's cabin, saved his boots, and chewed them into a pliable state. Later, as the survivors stood on the ice in the confusion just after the sinking, he noticed that her lips were cut in twenty places; she had endangered herself, suffered, and bled to save his feet. Later, his feet saved the party.

Nigeraurak, the cat, survived as well, along with three dogs and three puppies from the original twenty dogs alive when Bartlett started for Siberia.

Sixty years later, crew member McKinlay told his tale in Karluk: *The Great Untold Story of Arctic Exploration,* to set the record straight. Stefansson, in his account of the expedition, made no mention of the loss of eleven men.

Not everything gets said, and not everything that gets said gets said correctly. Even Captain Bartlett's words cannot be trusted. He says that Breddy died of an accidental shooting, though the circumstances and the report given by McKinlay indicate suicide or murder. He claims to be a teetotaler, but that was far from the truth. His dates waver, details blur; his embellishments carry his stories beyond fact or circle somewhere around the fact. Many of his papers and manuscripts have been lost; we will never be sure of what he knew, or what he intended us to know.

The written record cannot always be trusted. Already, in my reading, I had come across enough inconsistencies to know what Lady Franklin would not allow: Any written statement is as true as the awareness and the intention of the writer at that moment; and awareness is always shifting, the magnetic pole of the psyche following its own dark powers.

We painted our house yellow and planted daylilies.

Sam was born in Juneau. We named him for Samuel Nickerson, the first Nickerson child born in the New World—Cape Cod in the seventeenth century. Our ancestors on both sides were whalers.

When Sam was six and we visited the Alaska State Museum, near our house, he told me with assurance that every night at midnight all the animals woke up and went out into the mountains to play. I was convinced that it was so—that if we went there one midnight, we would find every diorama and display cabinet empty.

CHAPTER VIII

Stefansson and Rasmussen: Fragments

After Stefansson left the *Karluk* and traveled in the opposite direction east across the ice, he and his three companions (including Asatsiak, an Inupiat from Point Hope) encountered a cairn on the extreme northern tip of Prince Patrick Island, on June 15, 1915. It contained a message left by Leopold McClintock dated June 15, 1853, sixty-two years earlier, while on the Belcher expedition searching for Franklin. As Stefansson noted,

> There was a thrill about unrolling that damp and fragile sheet and reading the message from our great predecessor which had been lying there awaiting us more than half a century. We felt it as marvelous that his steady hand was so

legible after so long a time. It brought the past down to us, quite as wonderfully as it did for me five years later to talk in London with McClintock's wife, still hale and charming, and with his sons, and to be shown the manuscript diary of the day he wrote this message.

It was a rare moment of written connection in the emptiness of the Arctic and a corroboration of belief in the sanctity of the written word. In this case, the precious words did indeed come home, though they were not the last words.

Stefansson and his three companions left a message in a cairn a few miles south of McClintock's. It was found forty-six years later, in 1961, by a team of surveyors. In his autobiography, Stefansson notes: "It seems curious to me that tiny messages, a few inches long when rolled, can be found so easily in the vast expanse of the Arctic while a great expedition like Sir John Franklin's, with two ships and more than a hundred men, can be almost completely lost."

In spite of the *Karluk* and the cloud it cast over his career, Stefansson was not yet through with Wrangel Island. In 1921, he sent another expedition there to claim and occupy it for England. The party consisted of four white men, including Maurer of the *Karluk* expedition, and an Inupiat woman from Nome, Ada Blackjack, hired as seamstress. Blackjack, though competent with a needle, had never lived a subsistence lifestyle and knew nothing of hunting and trapping. When it became clear that a rescue expedition would have to be sent to retrieve them, one of the subscribers was Miss M. F. Gell, granddaughter of Sir John Franklin by his first wife, who had died during his expedition to Prudhoe Bay.

In September 1923, the rescue ship, *Donaldson*, reported in Nome that the four men had died; only Ada Blackjack survived—and Vic, the expedition cat, like Nigeraurak of the *Karluk*. Three of the men had left the island in a fatal attempt to get to Siberia. The remaining man, Lorne Knight, had died on the island of scurvy or a similar disease. Before he became totally disabled, he taught Blackjack to hunt and trap. What she was able to secure kept them going, and later herself. His legacy was a diary. Ada Blackjack, existing alone on Wrangel Island for almost two months, picked up where Knight left off and kept her own. She clearly stated that she wanted the facts known for Mr. Stefansson.

Blackjack's diary and Lorne Knight's diary became the sole documentation of the ill-fated colony. Except for a few pages written by one of the other three men, all diaries (even a duplicate set) of the lost men disappeared with them into the ice.

A curious battle over the written record and the reputation of Ada Blackjack ensued. Harold Noice, whom Stefansson had put in charge of the rescue operation from

Nome, provided a twisted story to the press, which he later recanted, claiming a nervous breakdown. The story accused Blackjack of everything from making improper advances toward the men to allowing Lorne Knight to die of starvation while she prospered. He had ripped out ten pages of Knight's diary. Later he produced them, but with erasures, blacked-out lines, and one missing piece. Stefansson struggled to right the story. But Blackjack was never truly doubted. She visited Knight's family in McMinnville, Oregon, where she was warmly received. They were convinced she had done everything in her power to help their son. And Blackjack went on with her life, helping her five-year-old son to recover from tuberculosis.

In the words of Inglis Fletcher, a friend of Stefansson's who spent time with her,

It seems a far cry from Lady Franklin, a product of a highly civilized time, to the so-called primitive Eskimo woman, Ada Blackjack.

Yet the same determination—the same single purpose was present in them both. In Lady Franklin, love for her husband was behind years of effort to unravel the mystery of his death, and justify his expedition. In Ada, left alone, love of her son kept her at her task of living—the same determination, the same steel-like quality and iron will kept these women to their self-appointed task. The force behind Ada's will to live was her mother instinct. She was determined to get back to Nome to see her five-year-old boy, Bennett.

So each, in her own way, worked for a single purpose—with no dissipation of energy, and in this lay their strength and success.

A curious coincident [sic] is in the fact that Captain Kellett, who was the first European to see Wrangel Island, was then in command of one of the ships of the Franklin search, sent out mainly through the efforts of Lady Franklin. So the history of these two women touched for a brief instant; two women who lived so many years apart—who were so unlike—and so alike in will and determination.

Their history touched too, of course, when Franklin's granddaughter subscribed to the rescue.

Even after the disaster of 1921–23, Stefansson was not finished with Wrangel Island. In 1924 he sent out yet another colonizing expedition, this one made up of one American and twelve Inupiats, including five women and five children. A baby was born on Wrangel Island. Within the year, the Russian ship *Red October* landed there, rounded up Stefansson's colonists, took them on board, and carried them to Vladivostock. Wells, the American leader, died there. The Inupiats were moved to Manchuria before finally being returned to Russia and then to Alaska. Two little Inupiat boys died along the way, one in Vladivostock and one in Manchuria. Their names were Billy and Hope.

The Russians took control of Wrangel Island once and for all, ending claims by Canada and the United States. Little is known of its uses since then, until recently, when it became a nature preserve. On the map, it marks the northern boundary of what has come to be known as Kolyma, the Arctic gold fields where millions—the exact number will never be known—of Soviet political prisoners disappeared between the 1930s and the 1950s. Though Solzhenitsyn gives little specific attention to it in *The Gulag Archipelago,* he says, "The Kolyma was the greatest and most famous island, the pole of ferocity of that amazing country of Gulag."

Stefansson left an impressive collection of works. He was driven to defend his theory that the Arctic is not inhospitable, and to defend his reputation as a man able to live well in that country. His books gave us the map of the archipelago that he wanted us to have, not one peopled by tragedies that he, at least in part, had set into motion.

Stefansson was followed by Knud Rasmussen, the Danish ethnologist, whose heart was purer. As Rasmussen traveled east to west across Canada and Alaska during his Fifth Thule Expedition (1921–24), he wove together strands of Franklin, Stefansson, and other Arctic explorers in a synthesis of old and new. His was the last record of some of the spokespersons of the ancient ways, the last picture, caught on film and paper, of a way of life vanishing into the moving ice.

Rasmussen made his enormous trek with two companions—Anarulunguaq, a twenty-eight-year-old Eskimo woman from Greenland, and Miteq, her cousin. During his expedition, he encountered Natives at Pelly Bay who provided accounts of the John Ross expedition of 1829, almost one hundred years before. On first sight, Ross's ship was taken to be a great spirit. When the ship sank in Lord Mayor's Bay, much of it was saved, and relics of it were still very much evident. (This was the expedition of 1829–33, during which John Ross's nephew, James Clark Ross, located the North Magnetic Pole, at 89°59′. After spending four winters ice-locked in the Arctic, the expedition was saved by a ship once commanded by John Ross, the *Isabella* of Hull.) Stories were told too of the Franklin expedition of 1845. One man related how his father and his hunting partners had come across three starving white men who had come from a large group whose ship had sunk.

Farther to the west, among the Netsilingmiuts, Rasmussen met several Eskimos who could recount, secondhand, the discovery of an abandoned ship from the doomed Franklin expedition. They told with some humor how the discoverers, ignorant of white men's ships, cut a hole inside below the water line, to look out, letting the water rush in. They also told how later that spring a boat was found with the bodies of six men inside it, along with knives, guns, and much food. Most significant, they told Rasmussen exactly where he might find bones.

There, on the east coast of the Adelaide Peninsula, in the exact place the Eskimos had indicated, Rasmussen found scattered bones and remnants of clothing from the Franklin expedition. He gathered them together and built a stone cairn above them, "hoisting two flags at half mast above; their own and ours. And without many words we paid the last honors to the dead." It was three-quarters of a century after the tragedy.

Cairns holding messages are yet to be found all over the Arctic. Sometimes there is no paper. Rasmussen tells the story of how he and a small band of inland Eskimos traveling south of Lake Hikoligjuag encountered a woman frozen in the snow. It turned out to be the wife of a man in his party. The woman had been lost the previous winter in a blizzard when she attempted to follow her husband, to assist him in getting to the next village for food. The man wept over her body, which was left where it was, but by the time the party got to their camp, he entered into the festivities with apparent happiness.

Loss and discovery rotate around the pole. When they merge there, like the meridians, then there is only one direction. We can call that place the Pole of Ferocity, the Pole of Inaccessibility, the Pole of Peace. Always it is the pole of ourselves. There, in stillness, we lose the urgency for documents and monuments, for markers along the way. The precious last words are known inwardly and clearly, beyond the coordinates of time and space, beyond the tortured jumpings of the compass needle.

Words are not only markers along the way. Monuments of fear, they can be obstacles to acceptance of ourselves as larger beings. As beacons of truth, they oscillate and cannot be trusted.

After the writer-in-residence program, I worked in a statewide prison education program. When that was closed for political reasons and I tried to reopen it, I was forced to a lawsuit—a contract suit against the State of Alaska. I had been blacklisted. Three years later I won my suit, which the state took to the Alaska Supreme Court. I then had to start again. At the Department of Fish and Game, I learned the politics of wildlife resource management and did what I could to protect and strengthen the conservation magazine I edited there. Now, after a battle of seven years, I was withdrawing, and I did not know if the magazine would survive. The front cover of my last issue carries the portrait of a porcupine; the back cover, a boreal owl.

The porcupine, whose mating calls are heard by hunters in the November woods, gives birth in March;

the single young porcupine is born with soft quills, which harden in an hour's time, enabling it to travel with its mother. The porcupine's slowness and ease of capture have saved the life of many a person lost or stranded in the woods. Far to the north, in the coldest of conditions, the small boreal owl, spotted as with flakes of snow, sings on the flanks of Mount McKinley. Two shy and singing animals that bring hope and succor.

CHAPTER IX

I Circle Back:
The Last Twenty Years

1972–1992

I was cleaning out my desk at work, soon to leave it forever. I opened the deep lower drawer to my right to look at the stacks of daily work journals, steno pads full of the hour-by-hour notes I had kept all these years. What to do with them? I had personal journals at home that would easily fill two such drawers.

I spent even more time than usual looking at the large wall map of the world that I had purchased for myself some years ago and that I had kept right beside me as I moved from workspace to workspace. Fortunately, these spaces, though small, always had a view of the mountains. It was there, looking out on Mount Juneau, that I first learned that evening darkness comes from the ground, not from the sky

—that shadows build up from the lowest point like rising water. In winter, the water rises frighteningly fast, until day and everything in it is drowned.

The wall map of the world was mine and would go with me. I had never kept personal photos or memorabilia on my desk. But I needed the map. The area of the Polynesian Kingdom of Tonga, which Martin and I once visited, was grimy. I had pointed it out over and over, drawn to the heat and blazing light of the South Pacific, the one place I have been where I felt no fear of being cold.

The only other personal property was a copy of Ezra Pound's translation of "The River Merchant's Wife: A Letter," my favorite poem. It was always near me, my truest map of travel and of separation. All else belonged to the office, with its random out-of-balance chairs and recycled metal desks. It could all go back to the huge state warehouse near the Coast Guard dock until some other worker not very successful in the capital needed a place to sit and work, a place to discover the nature of darkness and of light.

I threw out that last memo from Kent Roth. What would I accomplish by saving it? I remembered in Kazantzakis's *Saint Francis* the story of the young law student who dies and cannot climb up from the Inferno to Purgatory because he is so weighted down by pieces of his manuscripts stuck to him. I had to leave it all—no matter who or what took it over—and move on, free. Lady Franklin's theory, though it pulled me with great strength, was not my answer. I kept hearing Walt Whitman, singing back to me through the years: "You shall no longer take things at second or third hand . . . nor look through the eyes of the dead . . . nor feed on the specters in books." It was time to listen and filter, time to decide things for myself.

If the magazine was shut down for political reasons, as I knew was very likely to happen, so be it. I had done what I could. I had given it seven years. Seven is a charmed number. Now I had to travel on, and travel as light as I could.

It was the same at home. There were still the letters in my basement, the boxes of papers. Soon we would be leaving our house for the winter, turning it over to other people, friends who would be making it their own. It was time to clean out the clutter of more than twenty years. I was beginning to grasp what I had heard from Martin, the creed of sailors: Eventually you have to leave the harbor. You have to be free to fly at least to Purgatory. But how hard it was: notes in the wobbling hand of young children thanking me for poetry experiences—and their poems; school records; boxes and drawers of old manuscripts; kind words from friends or people I didn't even know; a faded copy in typescript of a 1934 translation recording the voyage of Malaspina to Alaska—one of my great treasures. And this was only the basement, where I worked. Upstairs and on the second floor were other wildernesses of records, unexplored, unnamed. Each drawer, each box, was a cairn containing, possibly, the critical document, or clues leading to the one that did. Yet I had never done a baby book for any of the children, not even the first, our daughter, Helen, who now had a daughter of her own.

Like members of the Franklin expedition, I would now have to drop possessions behind me: furniture, china, monogrammed silver, bedding, even books. *The Vicar of Wakefield* was one of the last Franklin possessions abandoned.

I had brought with me to Alaska everything I could. The car, a Plymouth Valiant purchased with our wedding checks, was crammed when I left Colorado with the children. We had arrived in October 1971. Just a year later, as I entered my second Juneau winter, the most famous Alaska disappearance occurred.

On Monday, October 16, 1972, a white and orange twin-engine Cessna 310 carrying U.S. House majority leader Hale Boggs, of Louisiana, and Congressman Nick Begich, of Alaska, flew out of Alaska's cold and icy skies. Boggs had come to Alaska to assist Begich in his bid for election to a second term. The campaign swing called for a trip from Anchorage to Juneau, just over five-hundred miles to the southeast. Twelve minutes into the flight, pilot Don Jonz radioed his flight plan. Nothing more was ever heard from the plane. Russell Brown, an aide to Begich, was also on board. Severe turbulence and icing conditions were reported in Portage Pass, southeast of Anchorage, at the time.

On October 17, the House of Representatives convened at twelve noon. The chaplain started his prayer with a line from Genesis: "The Lord watch between me and thee, when we are absent one from another." Tip O'Neill then explained the logistics: Bad weather was delaying the search, which would extend from Anchorage to Juneau, first over water, then over land. He ended on this note: "We have been informed that the pilot who was commanding the two-motor Cessna is one of the great bush pilots of the area. . . . It is our hope and prayer, of course, that the men will be found safe."

Hope, of course, was not enough. In spite of a massive search involving military aircraft, vessels, amateur radio operators, crack mountain rescue teams, and hordes of non-military searchers, no sign of the plane was ever found. From psychics to spy planes, from dreams to heat-sensing detectors, every possible method was used. As with the Franklin search, the coast was redrawn with new accuracy, but finally less was known of the fate of the Cessna 310 than of that of the *Terror* and the *Erebus*. Thick fog and bad weather hampered the search, which covered the coastline from Anchorage to Juneau but concentrated on two areas: the Portage Pass area and the wild mountainous area to the northwest of Juneau, between Juneau and Yakutat—the area of glaciers, the area of Lituya Bay.

Into the second week, the search expanded from fifty to sixty miles on either side of the flight path and as far south as two hundred and fifty miles below Juneau. At one point, debris spotted off Cape Fairweather gave rise to hope, especially since some of it was colored orange, but the debris turned out to be merely logs, pallets, and cardboard, apparently dumped by a passing ship. Another time, a block of ice caused hope.

As always happens, the story began to slip down to lower parts of the front page, and then, as of October 31, off the front page, to come back briefly on November 1 and thereafter be off. The focus of the story switched to the confusion over the November ballot: Nick Begich's name stayed on and he beat his opponent, Don Young. Young urged voters to cast their ballots for him, saying that if he won and Begich were found alive, he would resign. Boggs also won his election.

On November 24, the thirty-nine-day search was officially suspended. By November 28, the post mortem had begun. Estimates of search costs were placed at a million dollars. An Air Force spokesman said that most routine searches are conducted for ten to fourteen days but sometimes are extended if the search area is large. On November 29, petitions for presumptive death hearings for three of the missing men were filed; the Boggs family held out. On December 12, a special jury took less than twenty minutes to declare the three men dead.

On December 29, 1972, a little more than two months after the plane's disappearance, a presumptive death certificate was recorded. A memorial service was held at East Anchorage High School on January 7, 1973.

Politics in at least two states was changed by the disappearance, as was the course of families, friends, and colleagues. Twenty years have passed. No sign of the plane has ever been found. Twenty winters have swept over whatever clues might have been, covering them with more crystals of ice than can be comprehended. Millions of flight hours have been logged over the path of the lost plane. Nothing.

Nine years later, on July 18, 1981, a Cessna 185 carrying four people disappeared on a short flight from Little Port Walter to Sitka, in southeast Alaska. The plane is thought to have crashed on the rugged outer coast of Baranof Island. The pilot was Norman Riddell, of Anacortes, Washington. With him were his son, Randy, and daughter-in-law, Judy, and his son-in-law Rob Mourant, all of Juneau. An intensive search, including a U.S. Air Force photo reconnaissance plane, failed to turn up any evidence.

On September 1 of that year, another search was begun, for a missing Mooney 20E piloted by Buddy Reyner, of Las Vegas, Nevada, en route from King Salmon to Yakutat. The plane was last heard from when the pilot requested instructions on activating the runway lights at Yakutat. The search concentrated on the northwest shore of Yakutat Bay, from Point Manby to Disenchantment Bay. No sign was ever found.

On September 2, a Civil Air Patrol Cessna 180 carrying R. J. Lohman and R. J. Herman, who were searching for the missing Mooney, disappeared. On September 17, the Coast Guard suspended its search.

On September 25, the Coast Guard suspended a five-day search for Ed Maki and Danny Pardee, lost in their single-engine Aeronica Chief north of Haines.

One year after that, another plane—or perhaps two planes—vanished in what became one of Alaska's most mysterious disappearances. It was September 7, 1982, when Maria Iverson and her husband, Ben, flew into Anchorage from Hawaii, where they had been vacationing. Ben was to leave from Anchorage on a hunting trip, while Maria was to return to Juneau. But Maria knew something was wrong. Ben had been very nervous, and she had been having unsettling premonitions. Ben knew, she says, that he was not coming back. That night in the hotel in Anchorage, he took off all his jewelry except his wedding ring and gave it to her. At dinner, something he read in the paper upset him. He threw down the paper and left the table. She does not know what it was that he read, nor the reason for recent threats on his life. The next day they parted, Maria to return to their home in Juneau and Ben to prepare for his moose-hunting trip near Lake Clark. Maria was sure she would never see him again. Ben had said he really did not want to go.

On the night of September 9, Maria, in Juneau, had a vision—of a crash site. On September 10, she called Anchorage and was told a search had been started for Ben's plane. No one had informed her previously.

The search widened. Supposedly, the Cessna 180, equipped with floats, took off from Lake Hood in Anchorage bound for Lake Telequana, two-hundred miles to the west, at 6 P.M. in stormy weather. The plane was dark green with a white stripe. Its tail number was N2194Z. On board were Ben and his friend Tim Grierson, also of Juneau, and their pilot, Robert Books, Jr. They carried a red tent and a blue tent and bright yellow and blue raingear. The plane was last heard from as it flew into Merrill Pass. Strong winds and low ceilings obstructed the search. An Air Force C-130 flying at high altitudes failed to pick up signals from an emergency locator transmitter. Bad weather continued.

Maria pushed when the search flagged. She insisted that it go on. The Rescue Coordination Center at Elmendorf Air Force Base suspended its search in mid-September. It had logged 184 missions and more than 526 hours in the air. She went on, with family and friends. Ike Iverson and Al Grierson, brothers of the two passengers, coordinated the volunteer effort out of the Aero Flying Club in Anchorage, insisting that they would continue as long as there were volunteer funds. Pulling together reward money and pouring her own funds into the effort, Maria generated publicity. She asked all pilots within a 250-mile radius of Anchorage to be on the alert for the missing plane. Fliers were posted, ads placed. She hired helicopters, dog teams, snowmobiles, and guides. She spent time in the air herself. A psychic, Dorothy Allison of New Jersey, described a police officer who would help her and also a site that was important.

The officer turned out to be Wayne Walters, chief of police of Nenana, a town in between Anchorage and Fairbanks. Walters, now dead, claimed to have seen the plane on or about September 8. He and a friend observed the green-and-white-striped plane in the company of a plane with a totem pole design, taking on fuel at the Nenana airport. The crews put on board drums of fuel, one a fifty-five-gallon drum and other smaller ones. The fuel bill was signed by "Mr. Reed" of Lake Hood. The planes took off and were not heard from again. No Mr. Reed could ever be found.

Maria flew to the site Dorothy Allison had suggested, on Bear Paw Mountain. Nothing was found.

On December 3, 1982, not quite three months after the disappearance, a presumptive death hearing declared the men dead.

Exactly two years later, the plane was located, near the

intended original destination. It was completely cleaned out, with no broken glass or indication of a crash. It looked, Maria stated, as if it had been placed there, perhaps dropped by a helicopter, upside-down. A pistol belonging to the pilot and two pieces of bone were all the evidence found. The bone pieces may or may not have been human. No publicity surrounded the find.

For five years, twice a year, on Ben's birthday and on their anniversary, Maria would get long-distance calls with no voice at the other end. A sound like a train was in the background. Maria sees Ben in a Middle Eastern setting. She has had a consistent and vivid vision. As she says, "A vision never changes." She is sure he is in Iran, where he had spent time in the U.S. Army, or in Saudi Arabia. Recently she saw a newsclip of Saudi Arabia on television: It was the same site she has seen repeatedly in her vision.

September 1982 was a stormy month with numerous accidents and disappearances. Two Juneau residents, Robert Savikko and Erich Keskinen, disappeared while hunting south of Juneau in the Taku Inlet area. The Coast Guard search was suspended after several days when turbulence and high seas combined with discouragement. "There really wasn't any more to do," a Coast Guard spokesperson said. Savikko, a city assemblyman well known for public service, was honored with a beach park named in his memory.

On October 11, 1990, a twin-engine Aero Commander

carrying two U.S. Fish and Wildlife Service biologists and their pilot disappeared over the Arctic polar ice cap while the biologists tracked polar bears north of Barrow. The Canadair Challenger, with radar sensitive to the difference between metal and ice, joined in the massive search covering 300,000 square miles. Still, no trace was ever found. The two biologists, John Bevins, thirty-five, and George Menkens, thirty-three, were tracking bears equipped with radio transmitting collars and checking on cub survival rates. As the search began, spokespersons for the agency expressed hope. The weather was unusually warm and the men were equipped with survival gear. Bevins's wife, Julia, was quoted as saying, "I just hope I can still say I'm married when this is all over." They had been married three months. No clue was ever found.

It was a stormy day when I flew with the Civil Air Patrol from Anchorage to Valdez to take up my post as a spokesperson for the Department of Fish and Game after the *Exxon Valdez* oil spill. Snow was bulldozed into towering piles and aircraft were constantly overhead. Dead animals were gathered in drifts, waiting for necropsies, identification, and storage in refrigerated vans. Occasionally bags of them were thrown at our feet. It was, I figured, as close to a war zone as I would get. I learned to sleep where I could, eat when I could, use a bathroom if it was there. From a helicopter, with doors open on either side, I looked down on the gouged ship and saw the form of escaped oil: a broken, twisted rainbow.

Once, when Sam was four and walking with me through a Juneau parking lot, he tugged at my skirt and pointed to an oil puddle on the pavement. "Look," he said. "A rainbow died."

CHAPTER X

I Begin to Map the Present

What is it to stand on the border of that unknown land of disappearance, a terra incognita too large for any map? What happens when you come to know it is your own disappearance you fear and are compelled to map?

Introducing *Journal of a Solitude,* May Sarton says, "Begin here." It does not matter what you have done—or not done—in the past, only that you are aware now. De Long knew that, as he carefully chose concrete details that anchor his record in truth and meaning, details that illuminate it with radiance and carry it singing across the years.

It was July 2, 1992, just before the holiday weekend, and I had some time. It was now four weeks before my last day at the office, the day when I was to set out into empty

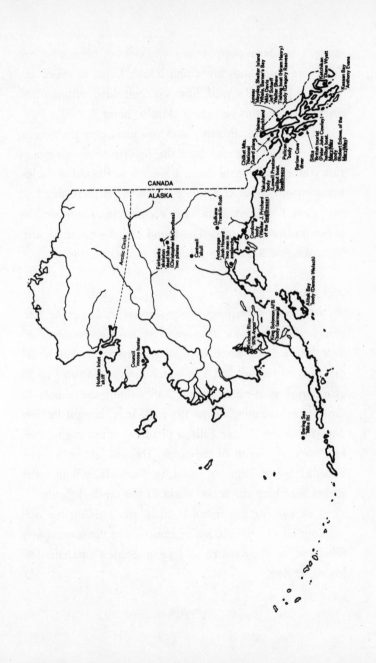

Juneau
(Whales, Farmer's Bay)
Shelter Island
(Herman Henry)
Milo Davis
Jeff Sonier
"Walter Shaw"
Fishing boat (Herman Henry)
(body) (Gregory Reeves)
Tenakee Springs
Dave Wyatt
Ketchikan
Kasaan Bay
Anthony Evans

Holmes

Chilkat Mts.
National
Guard plane

Yakutat
(body)
Jef Scharf
"Walter Frost"
SeaBreeze

Sitka
British tourist
(Peter John Cowley)
Twiller boat
Mary/May
(Robert Enloew, of the
Mary/May)

Barlow Cove
body

Pelican
"John Frost"
SeaBreeze

CANADA

ALASKA

Arctic Circle

Galkana
Franklin Roth

Cordova
Josh Howard
two men in
airplane

Fairbanks
skeleton
"Mad Trapper"
(Christopher McCandless)
two planes

Cantwell
skull

Anchorage
(Russell Preston)
Sarah Coleman

Altak Bay
body (Dennis Welsch)

Solomon AFB

Koyukuk River
90% Angel

King Solomon
(body Coleman)

Bering Sea
Mike Ihli

Council
moose hunter

Hotham Inlet
skiff

space. I had been postponing many tasks of organizing my departure from both office and house; I had to speed up. The day I set for myself, however, coincided with another disappearance, this one quite close to home.

In *Geographia*, Ptolemy says you must give precedence to observed phenomena over the reports of travelers and that you must compare the new records to the old to decide for yourself "what is credible and what is incredible." It was then I noticed a pattern, a connection between the paper trails and crumbs. The found and the eaten. Myself. My colleague Kent. The landscape of disappearance.

JULY 2

* *Jeff Scharff, a visiting twenty-year-old student at the University of Arizona, has disappeared on the Perseverance Trail near Juneau.* The search, involving thirty-five rescue workers, is in its second day. The search has concentrated on an abandoned gold-mine opening and along the shores of Gold Creek running below the trail. It is thought he may have fallen into Ebner Falls, a picturesque but raging falls in a narrow canyon of the creek. He was last seen there, outside his tent, listening to music. Particularly high water makes searching the rocky banks of the creek difficult.

This evening my friend Patricia, out walking the trail with our chocolate Lab, Kaleb, came across the search party filing out on their return to Juneau. Scharff's parents followed, crying.

JULY 6

The search for Jeff Scharff has been called off. It appears he drowned in Ebner Falls; his body lodged in one of the unstable, raging pools. The water is too volatile for further searching. A golden retriever named Josie, one of the Southeast Alaska Dogs Organized for Ground Search, or SEADOGS, was swept into the water by the falls and almost drowned.

✳ *Today, services were held for Milo Davis, skipper of the* Active, *a Juneau trawler that sank two weeks ago during a storm fifteen miles south of town.* His body has not been found. ✳ *Soon after the accident, the body of his nineteen-year-old crewman, Nick Plaskon, of Mill Valley, California, was found floating in a tangle of fishing gear and buoys.* Plaskon's body was found by the crew of the sailboat *Starstuff* while on the annual "Spirit of Adventure" race around Admiralty Island.

JULY 10

Edna Hulbert, a Chicago resident, has come to Juneau on a cruise ship to pursue her hobby—throwing bottles with messages into large bodies of water. Hulbert, at eighty-eight, is confined to a wheelchair but not about to stop the pursuit she began seventy years ago. Her messages, always starting, "Dear New Friend," have brought her many responses and begun many friendships. She claims that once, near Paris, she threw two bottles into the water. A young man found one and a young woman the other. Hulbert introduced them by mail, and they married.

I think of the only words of the Franklin party yet discovered, written on a standard Admiralty form used for sending messages in bottles from "discovery" ships and written in six languages. ("Discovery" ships were those sent out from England for exploration.) I think of the claim Captain Cook buried in a bottle at Point Possession, near Anchorage, and all the claims and messages placed by early searchers in bottles and in cairns and how they wait, still, to be discovered. The forward-thinking explorer Malaspina tried to simplify the claiming procedure by placing a coin instead of written testimony in a bottle, which was buried. I think of De Long's tomtit placed in a bottle off the coast of Brazil with a message for the *New York Herald*. The most wrenching bottle story of all is that of the discovery in 1849 of a bottle containing a message from Sir John Franklin. Imagine Lady Franklin's plunge from hope to despair when it turned out to be simply old news delivered to the sea in 1845 as the *Erebus* and the *Terror* set out.

It was a rule during the Franklin search that any party finding a monument was to dig in the ground ten feet true north to look for another message. Such double burial was intended to protect messages from possible removal by the Eskimo inhabitants. Sometimes cairns are disturbed and plundered. Captain Bartlett tells the story of looking for a cairn that Peary and his skipper left in the Duck Islands in north Baffin Bay in 1888. They each buried a fifty-cent piece as well as their records. When Bartlett dug out the cairn in 1926, the records and coins were gone.

I think of Hulbert's bottles and Franklin's messages, the searchers' messages, the wrecks of the *Jeannette* and the *Karluk* and the burned and broken whalers and the final words of all those sucked forever into the gyre of the polar drift, all flowing together in the green-white current—words, bones, and bits of wood, cast-off clothes, photographs, forks—all bumping against one another in the inevitable, grinding flow, clockwise and clockwise around the vortex of the pole, completing a cycle every two to four years through the necklace of frozen waters: the Beaufort Sea, the Chukchi Sea, the East Siberian Sea, the Laptev Sea, the Kara Sea, the Barents Sea, the Greenland Sea.

And how are we to know what and where is true north in a land where the compass swings? The magnetic pole itself moves—from a point on Boothia Peninsula, where James Clark Ross discovered it in 1831, to a point now just north of Bathurst Island, more than four hundred miles to the north and west. There is no visible sign to mark it. As Ross said, "Nature had here erected no monument to denote the spot which she had chosen as the centre of one of her great and dark powers."

And as for the pole, what is it to stand, as Peary did in 1909, at 89°57′ north, where there is only one direction—and still not be sure?

My friend Julie comes by to discuss some poems. *She recounts being on board* Starstuff *in the "Spirit of Adventure" sailboat race around Admiralty Island when it came across the body of Nick Plaskon, crewman of the* Active.

His open eyes were blue, she said. She cannot forget his open, staring blue eyes, the softness of his light brown hair and beard. He had been in the water about a day, buoyed by his lifejacket, tangled in gear. After the discovery of the body came the storm, with fifty-knot winds. One of the boats lost its mast. Others pulled out of the race. *Starstuff* kept going. During the mandatory layover at Baranof Warm Springs, however, the boat's cat was lost, and the crew dropped out in order to find it.

There at Baranof Warm Springs, in the general store, abandoned only a couple of years ago but largely taken back by the woods, Julie found a small journal. She showed me the little book, listing weather, needed groceries, letters mailed. A photograph of a man and a child is in the back, with some telephone numbers. The owner could be found but probably never will be. It is a series of found poems, but its owner is lost, disappeared into time, weather, circumstances.

I look at my journals—many in cloth, given to me by my children and by coworkers: flowers, cats, chintz, paisley, filled with my thoughts and the beginnings of many poems.

Some are full, written in to the last page, some not. Some, on their covers, are dated, some not. I have carefully saved them, my storehouse, my larder, my arsenal. Here are my favorite words, the images I horde. Why can't I drop them now, when my greatest need is to travel unburdened?

Julie is soon to leave to take a teaching post in Kenny Lake, near Glennallen, not far from Lake Louise, where recently a woman was mauled and eaten by a black bear. I look this place up in the *Dictionary of Alaska Place Names*. It is sixty-six miles northeast of Valdez, terminus of the oil pipeline.

In the *Dictionary of Alaska Place Names*, there are no places named Disappearance but numerous ones named Discovery. And ships, too, named *Discovery* appear, disappear, and reappear. One *Discovery* first served Cook and then later brought his former midshipman, George Vancouver, to southeast Alaska on two voyages between 1792 and 1794. Attention focuses on Vancouver now because of the bicentennial of his expeditions, which named many places in the area where I live. We have these names because of *Discovery*. In 1875, when the Admiralty determined to reach the North Pole, they sent out George Nares on *Discovery*.

Another *Discovery* was the steamer carrying freight that disappeared with all hands (twenty-four) at the entrance to Lituya Bay in November 1903. Her passengers had all fled at Unga and Kodiak, claiming the boat was not seaworthy.

Chief John of the Lituya Bay Indians is said to have watched her for an hour foundering at the entrance to the bay.

JULY 13

Today, after several days of rain, the mountains have disappeared in fog. The lupines are almost gone. Fireweed is rampant, and the tall flowers of late summer—delphinium, stock, foxglove, lily—are all bending in the rain.

I have noticed how foxglove packs up for the winter from the ground floor, shedding the lowest blossoms first. Finally there are only a few blossoms left, swaying precariously from the top of the stalk—survivors reaching out from an attic, waving for help. It is the attic of the wind.

My younger son, seventeen-year-old Sam, has come out of the Alaska Range, far to the north, where he has been learning to ice-climb on glaciers. He was taking a course with the National Outdoor Leadership School as a graduation present, in the transition before college. His brother Tom, twenty-four, has gone into other mountains, in Washington. Tom reappears, with sea kayakers, on Orcas Island, calls, then goes off again with his group into the wilderness. To be the mother of mountain climbers takes special faith—to be sure of the kindness of the rocks, the goodness of the earth, the steadiness of hand and foot. I think of the relatives of all on the Franklin expedition and on countless other polar expeditions. Many of those who walked into the ice were boys. Captain Bartlett of the *Karluk* was fond of repeating the Newfoundland proverb "The sea is made of mothers' tears." Sandy Anderson, the *Karluk*'s mate who vanished, was "not yet twenty-one."

Places of mystery appear, disappear. My friend John, the department's photographer, tells me of a lava tube off St. Lazaria Island, near Sitka. Twelve feet wide and approximately five hundred feet long, it is a conduit for seals, but no diver has dared to go its length. Each has turned back as the tube has narrowed, but the seals do not turn back.

The Tlingits tell the migration story of the Killer Whale Clan, Duxawadey. As the clan moved south down the Stikine River from Alaska's interior, it encountered a glacier which blocked its way. Two brave women asked permission of the clan leader to explore a route beneath the glacier. Granted permission, they made a raft of tree branches covered with swans' down, and on this raft they floated under the glacier to emerge safe on the other side.

To the Tlingits, the glacier is endowed with spirit life, *sit-tu-yhage*. This spirit is manifested in cold wind. In Juneau, bubbles of this cold wind break off from the icefields above the city and spill down the mountainsides in a weather phenomenon known as the taku. The taku can blow at high and fierce rates for hours or even days on end.

It is not surprising that the Tlingits imbued glaciers with great power and sometimes tried to propitiate them by throwing dogs or slaves into crevasses; rotting flesh was meant to drive them back. Glaciers know an endless hunger. Day by day they grow in depth, grinding their way inexorably toward the sea, some in a sudden hurry.

JULY 17

✳ *The body of the captain of a boat that capsized on the Kvichak River on July 4 has been found.* Earlier, the boat and the body of a crewman were found off Graveyard Point, on the Bristol Bay coast. The boat is the *90% Angel,* and I think of Angel, the student at Sam's school who disappeared into the Parker River in Massachusetts just before baccalaureate—how Angel and this captain are together now, percentages and all measurements of division gone. And I think of how Captain Bartlett had a nephew named Jack Angel who sometimes sailed with him as engineer and photographer, and how Bartlett's manuscripts and photographs are now scattered, his plans for literary monuments lost, his tracks filling in with time.

The Kvichak River heads in Lake Iliamna, near Naknek, in the Bristol Bay region of southwest Alaska. Lake Iliamna, one of Alaska's largest lakes, has long been a source of stories of mystery, disappearance, and monsters. It is the place where Hieromonk Juvenaly disappeared in 1795, leaving the story of a barefoot priest running into the snow.

The stories, continuing, include alleged sightings by bush pilots and anglers of an Iliamna monster or "mystery fish." Old stories persist of a monster eating boats—but only red-bottomed ones—and of huge holes found in subsistence gill nets. Large sturgeons, seals, and beluga whales, which occasionally swim up the Kvichak River from Bristol Bay, are all possible explanations, but the campfire stories continue. Lake Iliamna has depths in excess of one thousand feet.

Vastness gives way to mystery. Disappearance takes on larger dimensions. Along the Alaska Highway, in Watson Lake, British Columbia, Johnnie Friend's pigs disappeared one night from a fortresslike enclosure. What could have carried them off? The name Sasquatch returns. Strange sounds are heard nearby. My friend John, the photographer, has camped there and heard them. He has told me.

JULY 23

✳ *Walter Shaw, a seventy-two-year-old visitor from Vero Beach, Florida, was reported missing from the* Sagafjord *four hours after it left Juneau.* His wife, Jean, said he had left the ship, moored in Gastineau Channel, to mail some postcards. She did not realize he was missing until after she had waked from an afternoon nap and the ship was under way. He may or may not have gotten off the tour ship before it departed. Shaw, the retired president of the Turner Corporation of New York, suffers from occasional mental lapses.

"It's very strange," a cruise ship spokesperson was quoted as remarking. "This [Juneau] is a small town. You just don't disappear here." The population of Juneau is about twenty-eight thousand. There are no roads in or out.

JULY 25

It is Saturday, the last Saturday before I retire, on the coming Friday. I am at the office, finishing up what I can— it seems insurmountable. Sam is running in a race up the Mount Roberts trail. Clouds obscure the mountains. From my office window, looking at them, I can barely make them out. I am listening to National Public Radio's *Weekend Edition*. The host, Scott Simon, is talking about how he, at age forty, is going to leave for a year to do another network's weekend program. He thanks the people at NPR with whom he has been working. As you go through transit points, he says, you should tell the people who are important to you that you love them.

I throw out more papers, decide that so many more letters will go unanswered forever: a thicket of connections missed and severed, messages lost.

Repeatedly, I think of Thomas Hardy, a favorite author, whose plots so often hinge on a letter not received.

JULY 31

It is my last day at the office.

Already I have thrown out what must be a half-dumpster-load of paper. Now I confront the final stacks, the last written records of what has been my world. I have been up almost all night and am exhausted and discouraged. How could I have left so many loose ends? So many papers not dealt with—I, who pride myself on efficiency?

As the hours rush by, I toss more out. It mustn't be left as baggage for whoever follows. My supervisors have not yet hired a replacement for the position—a bad sign, one that spells lack of commitment to the magazine.

A fellow worker asks me what I have learned, and I can think of nothing serious to say, only "Beware of the pillar," an absurd sign I once saw on an interior pillar in the office of a Seattle acupressurist who cured me of pleurisy. I don't know whether that is because I am so tired, because I feel afraid to make a pronouncement, or because I really don't have anything to say after all these years. Maybe the great lesson is silence; but maybe that is the Hermit reversed— withdrawal, aloneness, inability to act. In a daze, I get through the day and two surprise parties given by fellow workers, celebrations that fill the day with happiness and sadness.

I leave the little community of battered chairs—the stained orange one, the low blue one—to return to my one-armed brown chair in the basement at home, which I keep covered with a quilt or a blanket. As a child, I was brought up in a beautiful house, surrounded by beautiful things. I sat in venerable chairs, most with a long and distinguished past. Now the beautiful things I own, for the most part, are in a mini-storage unit in Smithtown, New York, four thousand miles away. They have been cached. The plan was to pick them up later, but who can tell the route?

I have a growing hunger for beauty. As Kazantzakis has Saint Francis say, "The only way we can divine the appearance of God's face is by looking at beautiful things."

Helen and her daughter, India, have flown in from New York, joining Tom and Sam. We are all together for this time of transition, a time so busy I cannot step back to see it. There are parties and toasts, and an amazing quietness that follows on that first Monday morning, when I hold in my hands the gifts that have been given me, including a mock issue of the magazine. I can watch and listen more closely now. I can stick the flags of disappearance on the map I am making. I can watch it fill up, take shape. I remember my maternal grandmother's house in Water Mill, and the attic, reached by folding stairs lowered from a trapdoor. There, a huge map of World War II Europe lay spread on a table with colored pins to mark troop movements. One uncle had been in the army. Later he had become a monk. Then he married, had four children—cousins I did not know.

AUGUST 3

The search for Shaw continues, with no clues. A private investigator has been hired by the family. Fliers with color photographs are posted about town. During an interview,

Peter Shaw, his son, said of the disappearance, "It is the kind of thing that happens to someone else."

The mountains are hidden in fog. The sound of migrating geese comes through the clouds and through the open window.

At the top of the state, in Barrow, the place where the whalers used to be caught as prey by the ice, the sun has set for the first time this summer. In their season, it would have been time for the whalers to be leaving. In a bad year, it might already be too late.

I notice the foxgloves, their stalks ever emptier as blossoms drop from all but the very top. They are climbing to winter. Now even the fireweed, in its wild sweep of red and purple, fades: the last brave flag of summer.

As I see the fliers for Walter Shaw posted around town, I remember my fellow Bryn Mawr College student Kathy Boudin, whose face I saw for some years on post office bulletin board "most wanted" sheets. One of the Weathermen, she was captured and now spends her life in prison, another kind of disappearance. My roommate Caroline used to argue politics with Kathy, who lived just down the hall. She would argue vigorously, long after I was exhausted. Caroline also argued with Bryn Mawr. She wanted to spend her junior year in Lebanon but was not allowed. Kathy, however, was permitted to go to Moscow. I was busy studying English literature, focusing on the Romantic period and in love with Victorian novels. Caroline was one of my bridesmaids. Now I have not seen her for twenty years.

✳ *In Barlow Cove, north of Juneau, a young diving student runs out of air thirty feet from the surface, grabs for her partner's mouthpiece, knocks his mask off, and, in the scuffle, disappears.* Ten minutes into the Coast Guard search, her body floats to the surface.

One of Juneau's most famous hunting guides, Karl Lane, disappeared while diving in Hawaii. He had heart trouble. He was diving alone. He undoubtedly did not want to be found. He who had been hunter would not be prey.

AUGUST 8

Walking on the boat dock in Douglas, across the Gastineau Channel from Juneau, Tom and Sam and I, being silly with a rented video camera, come across *Starstuff.* The ship's cat, the one that temporarily disappeared at Baranof Warm Springs during the race, sits in the late evening sun next to the boat. We stop to talk to her, examine her tag. Her name, we discover, is Pandora. She is striped and soft. No crew could bear to leave her behind. And what is a race to Pandora, who has interests and concerns of her own? She enjoys our attention but does not follow us as we leave.

At home, I consult my encyclopedia to refresh my memory of Pandora: the first woman, sent by Zeus to earth with a dowry in a box—all human ills and sorrows. When the box was opened, all these evils escaped into the world. Only hope was trapped, ever after to cheer and cheat mortals.

Is hope the engine that propels us, the silver cord that ties soul to body? What enables hope to live so long in the north? Is it tied to the "great dark powers" of the magnetic pole restlessly moving beneath the surface?

I remember *Pandora*, which became *Jeannette*, only to disappear into the polar ice.

I remember Nigeraurak, the *Karluk*'s cat, and Vic, the cat that kept Ada Blackjack company on Wrangel Island.

And I remember Captain Bartlett's story of the witch cat. On a fishing boat out of Labrador, he had a black cat on board. Bad weather persisted and the boat could not fish. One of the crew, a crotchety old man, blamed the cat. The cat disappeared and the weather improved dramatically. The other crew members accused the old man of throwing the cat overboard. It would come back to haunt him, they said. Soon after, the old man pulled the dead body of the cat up with a haul in his net. Within a year, he was dead.

AUGUST 10

Helen and one-year-old India have left. I watched their plane head south, then make the graceful arc slightly to the west, toward the Pacific Ocean—that largest place on earth.

I noticed then the trailing flowers, the raggedy hem of late summer—last lilies, last daisies. Did I tell them, children and flowers, that I love them?

I remembered "The River Merchant's Wife: A Letter," and its last lines, which sing across twelve hundred years and the quagmire of translation:

> The leaves fall early this autumn, in wind.
> The paired butterflies are already yellow with August
> Over the grass in the West garden;
> They hurt me. I grow older.
> If you are coming down through the narrows of the river
>   Kiang,
> Please let me know beforehand,
> And I will come out to meet you
>   As far as Cho-fu-sa.

Its author, the eighth-century Chinese poet Li Po, is famous for having dumped a basket of poems in a river as well as for his poems that survived. He did not need to hold on to his words, but still they have found us. Generation after generation they find us, showing us the way. The way is waterfall; moss at the gate; a lone sail disappearing on a river that reaches to heaven. And that is why the poem, which knows no barriers, is always in the present and is, as Ezra Pound says, the news that stays news.

* * *

Language disappears. Twenty of Alaska's Native languages are in danger, according to articles that appear. In their pioneering linguistics work, Richard and Nora Dauenhauer put it more strongly. Of Alaska's twenty-one languages, they state, only two, Central Yupik and Siberian Yupik, are still being learned by children. Of Tlingit speakers in southeast Alaska, only a few are younger than sixty. The Alaska Native Language Center at the University of Alaska in Fairbanks brings forth a collection of Denaina (Athabaskan) stories collected by Peter Kalifornsky, a resident of Kenai and one of the last storytellers of the Kenai branch of the Tanaina people. He is the only writer now working in the dialect. The university is offering, for the first time, certificate and associate degrees in Athabaskan language education, hoping to meet the demand for qualified Athabaskan language teachers. Sheldon Jackson did his work well, seeking to obliterate Native languages; and the Alaska Department of Education seems not to be concerned with reversing the trend.

In Juneau, the summer days continue, though we know they are short in number. The weather reports note the loss of daylight each day—two minutes, three minutes, five minutes—but we are still a month from the equinoctial storms that blow in from the gulf, lifting the seas ten feet, twenty feet, thirty feet.

There is no more discussion of the young hiker who disappeared on Perseverance Trail. Hundreds upon hundreds of other hikers have passed by the place where he stepped off the trail and out of sight, but there are no clues.

At 9:30 one evening last week, Sam hoisted a heavy pack and ran along the Perseverance Trail to Granite Creek Basin, reaching his campsite just as it grew dark. I do not know if he wondered, as he passed Ebner Falls, about the fate of that young man.

Around town, the fliers for the missing tourist, still advertising the $5,000 reward, begin to disappear. There has been no comment on the story for some time.

There is no more word about Kent Roth and his brothers and friends who disappeared in their plane out of Yakutat. If Land Otter Men have taken them home, they must be found quickly or not at all. But who knows where to look? The compasses dance; the crevasses contract; the glaciers move forward, eating what falls in their jaws; and wind blows the indiscriminate snow over everything in its path.

The great brown bears, slaves to the Spirit of Lituya Bay, roam the outer coast. Their hunger increases now, as they sense the coming winter and the long months in hibernation.

Twenty years later, the search for Nick Begich and Hale Boggs is to be resumed, to a limited extent. A newspaper in Washington, D.C., *Roll Call,* has published a story based on FBI documents. The documents indicate that the government received information through sophisticated tracking devices that the plane had been found in Icy Bay, near Yakutat, and that there were two survivors. The Begich family was never told.

Hundreds of feet of snow will have fallen, but there is new hope that the site can be located.

Hope has dragged endless searchers through the far north, kept them going to the end, taken them into the silent ice. "Hope" is a frequent word in their journals. It spills out on maps. One of the first places found and named in the far north was Hold-with-Hope Peninsula, on the eastern coast of Greenland, discovered by Henry Hudson in 1607. But perhaps the only one who got it right was Dr. Elisha Kent Kane, the American explorer who was part of the Franklin search. In a desperate attempt to break free from his ice prison on the Greenland coast, he once set out for help in a whaleboat named *Forlorn Hope*.

AUGUST 11

Far to the north, the mountain my son Tom climbed at eighteen—and North America's largest—is claiming an unusual number of lives. The National Park Service has announced that it has spent $206,000 this summer rescuing climbers and removing bodies from Mount McKinley during its deadliest season ever. Eleven climbers have died and numerous parties have had to be rescued. Questions have become louder about whether taxpayers should carry the cost of rescuing mountain climbers, especially foreigners, who represented all but one of the deaths this season. The NPS pays about $180,000 a season to have a high-altitude helicopter standing by, whether or not it is used. It also pays climbers already on the mountain eighteen dollars an hour to help with rescue efforts. This year, however, the Alaska Army and Air National Guard helped more than they have in the past. In spite of the unusual rescue efforts, the total cost was about the same as it was last year, when there were no fatalities and half as many rescues. Restrictions on who might climb would be impractical, Park Service personnel maintain. The only American who died on the peak this season was Mugs Stump, a veteran Alaska mountain guide and one of the country's foremost mountaineers, who fell into a crevasse on May 21.

Mount McKinley rescues pale by comparison with other search-and-rescue efforts statewide. During 1991, the seventeenth U.S. Coast Guard district, which encompasses the State of Alaska—with 33,000 miles of coastline and 3,853,500 square miles of water for search-and-rescue operations and another 950,000 square miles for law enforcement—launched 1,192 rescues and reported 45 fatalities. The unsuccessful search for Kent Roth's plane involved 900 hours of flight time, including military flight hours.

I discuss with Tom this question of rescue: How much should be done? Who is to be responsible? There are, after all, those who choose to disappear. On February 5, 1992, thirty-four-year-old Dee Lacy, of Juneau, left a note telling her husband she was going on a hike and would return later that day. She did not return. An intense search ensued, taking six days, involving sixty searchers, requiring thousands of person-hours and $9,500 in expenses. Volunteer searchers gave up days at work and provided personal expenses. They tracked with dogs, searched coastlines on foot and by boat, flew helicopters in bad weather, operated radio communications and computers, queried bus passengers, drew sketches and provided maps, and made and delivered food to searchers.

Five days after the search began, there was a report that Lacy was alive in another southeast town. Later she told a newspaper reporter that she was sorry about the incident but that she was suffering from amnesia and could not remember what had happened. Family members gave their versions of the story. Nothing was clear, except for one fact. Lacy was troubled. She had moved to Juneau only three months before, soon after a second marriage, and was experiencing both financial and personal problems.

Soon after revelation of the hoax, a Juneau state senator introduced legislation requiring those who cause unnecessary searches to be financially liable for the costs incurred.

A month later, a young Juneau man, Tony Prater, disappeared. He was a friend of Tom's. He had gone hiking on Mount Jumbo on a nice Saturday in March. An Australian and an outdoorsman, he knew his way around the mountains. He was not declared missing by his friends until Wednesday. Soon after the search was launched, his body was found at the 1,600-foot elevation. Whether he could have been saved if found earlier cannot be known, but days of what could have been vital time passed before his friends notified authorities. Tom, in Anchorage, was distraught. He could not understand why there had been such a delay.

An elementary school student named Rusty Dursma disappeared some years ago on Mount Juneau with a friend when the two decided to play hooky and go up the mountain instead of to school. I watched the search from my bedroom window, the orange-vested searchers fanning out over the mountain. When he was found, by a local doctor, he had been dead only a short time. He had fallen into a crevice, broken a leg, and died of hypothermia. He had been a classmate of Tom's; and two other contemporaries and neighbors of Tom's died young, one drowning in Auke Lake, one drowning in Gold Creek. A third died of a brain tumor.

Tom reached the top of McKinley soon after he turned eighteen. That night—the night of the summer solstice—Martin was on a sailboat in the "Spirit of Adventure" race. There was a terrible storm Martin's year, not as bad as this year, but bad enough. At home, wind tore at the trees in a greenish light. All night our dog howled. There was nothing I could do to comfort him, nothing. I did not know until much later that Tom, in the exhaustion of oxygen deprivation, was summiting the mountain that night and that Martin was struggling with icebergs and wind: two family members pushed to extremes.

The dog who would not be silent—faithful and difficult to the end—is long gone. Still, I continue to mourn him: Boy.

Martin had retired two years earlier and had the sailboat of his dreams, *Monomoit,* waiting for him in the
West Indies. He had sailed her there, over many
months, from Maine. Now that I had reached early retirement age as well, I could join him. We were going
to live on board for the winter. It was a dream, but
there were hazards and difficulties. I was not a sailor.
Given my choice, I would have taken to a horse instead.

But our home for the winter would be English
Harbour, Antigua, former base of Admiral Lord Nelson, that most celebrated and most reckless of British
admirals. Christopher Columbus, who visited the island
in 1493, named it for a church in Seville. Nelson com-
mandeered English Harbour as the best hurricane hole

in the eastern Caribbean. From there he was able to hold sway over the watery empire of the West Indies; the ships of other nations had to flee during hurricane season. *Monomoit* was tied up there now in a mangrove swamp—the safest place in a storm.

CHAPTER XI

One Almost Lost

Knocks at My Door

1992: AUGUST 12–AUGUST 29

AUGUST 12

It is Martin's birthday, his fifty-second, and his second year of retirement from his state job at the Department of Transportation. He moves out further in front of me past the great meridian.

I am reminded how the 180th meridian, the one that carves the world in two and separates longitude into east and west, passes through Alaska. The international date line zags away from it, indeed, in order not to split the state into different days. I am reminded also how maps can deceive, especially in regard to the far north and the far south. The poles invite distortion. The Mercator projection, in fact, requires it. Alaska, even now, is often shown in very reduced size to fit onto the page, sometimes in a box in the Pacific Ocean south of California or sometimes as a larger, fabulous land cutting across Mexico: a place Texans might consider easy to reach. It is no wonder so many Americans fail to recognize Alaska as part of the union.

In the past, astronomers have "discovered" moons that were not there, and hydrographers have charted islands that were not there. Now we chart stars so far away we cannot see them; we sense them by radio waves, by indirect information. Some "lost" islands have persisted on the charts for years. Los Jardines, for which La Pérouse was searching on his way to Botany Bay and beyond, doggedly hung on from the sixteenth century until well after World War II. The Auroras, for which Malaspina searched after leaving the coast of Alaska, faded faster, by 1825. Where have these fabulous islands gone? The Islands of the Blessed? The home of the Hyperboreans? What has happened to the notes of failed astronomers, geographers, and hydrographers, the chartmakers who set the ship-swallowing dragons in the unknown oceans of the old maps? Are they weighted down by their scribblings, unable to shake themselves free?

✳ *This morning on the radio I hear that three crew members from a sinking fishing boat near Juneau have been rescued. One of them is Hiram Henry, a friend of Sam's.* An hour later, out walking the dog, I meet Hiram on a bicycle, coming across the bridge. Not sure he is Hiram, whom I have not seen in a couple of years, I give him only a perfunctory greeting. Back home, I hear that Hiram has been at the house looking for Sam, away on a camping trip in Skagway. I want to retrace my steps and embrace him, tell him how glad I am that he is Hiram, not a ghost. But Hiram is now far off on his bike, in search of other friends, perhaps now appreciating his friends as never before, perhaps filled with a sense of joy and compassion he cannot understand.

The literature on near-death experiences grows. The detractors, holding to similarities with hallucinogenic drug trips, fail to grasp that the near-death experience is nearly always positive, and nearly always leads to a transformation for the better. As fear of death falls away, love of life increases, and compassion. There is no death of consciousness. There is no end. There is only transition. Those who have crossed the border of disappearance and returned know this and are at peace.

There is indeed no "disappearance," which the dictionary says is extinction. There is only a changing, something for which we do not yet have a name, a moving into different form; it is something like "transpearance," something we have yet to define. We are lacking symbols, legend. Here it looks like one thing, there another. If we could name it, we would have less fear; but first we must learn to let go of what we have—words, symbols, maps.

I cannot do that yet. Hermit, cartographer, I am still trying to wrestle life down on the page, making it fit, shaping it into a portrait. My tool is fear—false evidence taken as truth; and it is a sharp, precise tool. I am the ancient chartmaker decorating my seas with ship-swallowing serpents. Carefully, methodically, I am filling the empty spaces with totems of fear. I will not give up words, these messages that might mean survival. If I set these records down, I might be found—and saved.

Tonight, on the radio, more news. Another discovery and another disappearance. ✳ *A Sitka fisherman, fishing near Pelican, pulled up the remains of what appeared to be a fisherman in yellow raingear.* The remains, caught on a one-sixteenth-inch steel cable, quickly slipped off and disappeared back into the water, where sharks are reported. The Coast Guard, when notified, flew over the area, consisting of hundreds of miles of open water. Since there were no reports of missing boats or people, they decided a search would not be feasible. Sometimes the book of the ocean opens, only to shut quickly again.

On June 22, the F/V *Provider* was fishing for scallops east of Cape Yakataga, along Kent's route, when the crew pulled up something heavy, which fell out of the net before it reached the surface. One crewman said it was an aluminum airplane. No positive identification could be made.

Sometimes it can be calculated where a body will turn up. It is a question of tides, currents, water temperatures, and local conditions. Bodies of those who fall off the Juneau dock usually turn up across the channel on a beach on Douglas Island. *No remains of Walter Shaw have been found, however.* The ship he traveled on has returned to Juneau many times, and many other tourists, full of hope for their journey, have inhabited his cabin, slept in his bed, not knowing his story, as it slowly disappears.

The weather has turned autumnal, with dark, heavy clouds.

We celebrated Martin's birthday last night, going out to dinner, because Tom was scheduled to leave this morning. Often we have been blessed with rare good weather on this date and have been able to celebrate out-of-doors, in the front yard. I remember one especially beautiful birthday celebration just before Sam was born, when Martin and Tom had just returned from Tenakee Springs, where they had been crabbing, and another when Tom was nineteen and had shot a deer on Mount Jumbo and I cooked a huge venison roast for a large group of friends. I remember those precious occasions—friends, abundant good food, an enormous cake, and our laughter alive on the lawn until the sun, heavy in its sinking arc, slips behind the mountains on Douglas Island and we are forced to abandon the crabapple tree and the giant black willow to the rising flood of darkness and cold.

Our neighbor Charlie McLeod has told us the history of the willow that dominates our yard and house. His father, one of the early lighthouse keepers here, brought its parent with him from Edinburgh and planted it in Evergreen Cemetery, where so much of Juneau's history lies. One summer night at about this time, Tom, standing in the yard surveying the neighborhood for a bear that was reported, heard a scratching and looked up; the black bear was in the willow, over him. I had just said goodbye to an old family friend who had been in Juneau for a short visit on a tour ship. After dinner on the ship with her, I drove her around town, promising that a bear would appear suddenly. She missed the bear, left for Skagway, and has long since died: Helen Dartt.

AUGUST 14

✳ *Today the Coast Guard reports a search launched near Shelter Island, close to Juneau, in response to a Mayday call from a vessel reporting to have ten children on board.* A Coast Guard spokesperson commented that occasionally fraudulent calls are received: "We've had a few in recent months, and spent man-hours and taxpayer money on calls that turned out to be nothing. But if someone calls in for help, we don't dismiss it as a hoax. We treat it as a true Mayday immediately and send out our resources."

AUGUST 15

We are up at 3:15 to launch Martin and Sam on a fishing trip.

This morning, in heavy rain, a friend is to lead a pack of Cub Scouts to Granite Creek Basin, along the Perseverance Trail, where Jeff Scharff disappeared. The trail, a favorite one in Juneau, is heavily used; it gives quick access from the city to the extraordinary views of the mountains and valleys leading east to Canada. It runs to the site of the old Perseverance Mine, first claimed in 1885.

Granite Creek Basin, a couple of miles off the Perseverance Trail, is the destination Sam made the other night. It is a wildly beautiful bowl in the mountains with a roaring waterfall and the loud chorus of marmots. It is a place of solitude and power. I have been there only once. I always seem to have too much work, too much paper to deal with, to get out and hike. I depend on others to tell me, to remind me, of what is there in the soaring mountains.

Wind and rain are to increase over the next two days. Already the trees are bending deeply. There is a heaviness and darkness in the air.

AUGUST 16

It is the day when Sir John Franklin saw, named, and quickly left Prudhoe Bay in 1826. For him, winter had already come. He would not meet Beechey at Point Barrow. He would have to return to the Arctic to complete the small gap now left in mapping the Northwest Passage. He would have to come back and be lost before the explorations could be realized.

In a strange footnote to the missed connection between Beechey and Franklin that day, in 1849 one of the Franklin search ships discovered a cask of flour buried by Beechey twenty-three years before and held a celebration featuring cakes and pastry made of Beechey's flour.

In 1976, Roderic Owen, a descendant of Franklin's, flew to Prudhoe Bay from England to unveil a plaque commemorating the hundred and fiftieth anniversary of the explorer's discovery.

I know something of what he saw from the air. It is a strange experience to fly over the polar ice cap. We did it from Anchorage in 1977 on our way to London to visit relatives during the Queen's Silver Jubilee. We were on a British Airways 747. A steward invited Sam, then two, up to the cockpit and took him away. When some time had passed and I felt anxious, I went in search. I will never forget reaching the top of the spiral staircase leading to the cockpit. I looked through the open door, over the instrument panel, out the window of the plane's nose. There was no one there—nothing to obstruct the view of the blinding ice, an immensity of frozen white. When my shock had subsided, I looked down and to the right. There was Sam, under the care of the flight engineer, "playing" with the computer. I scooped him up and returned to our seats, hoping that the pilot and the copilot would soon finish with their social calls. It is not so casual on planes anymore, but I was given a view for all times: that invisible servant autopilot, leading its party across the place where the lines of navigation disappear.

✳ *Today a search is begun in Sitka for a British tourist who was last seen a month ago at a Sitka trailhead.* When Peter John Cowley, thirty-five, stopped calling and writing home, his father, in London, reported him missing, then traveled to Sitka with a family friend. A Sitka resident who saw a picture of the missing man in the local newspaper told police he gave Cowley a ride to the Mount Verstovia trailhead on July 10. The U.S. Coast Guard plans to assist in the search with helicopters. Again. Again.

I decide to review recent Coast Guard searches. Flipping through search-and-rescue news releases at the Coast Guard headquarters in the federal building in Juneau, I quickly find a terrible sameness to the stories. The reports usually continue for three to five days. If the case is large, or unusual, reports continue for a week or even two weeks. Then, for the most part, there is a blankness. Sometimes, at a later date, a body is found, or a boat, but most often there is no further reference, no end to the story. The news releases pile up, file after file, drawer after drawer, a paper snow of loss and mystery. Earlier files have already been taken away, stored in Washington, D.C., a more remote burial ground of mystery and of loss, years of blizzards burying every clue. An accumulation that merges into a glacier of statement, impersonal and blunt.

✳ JUNE 10, 1992: The USCG suspended its search for two men whose skiff was found overturned off Kodiak Island Tuesday.

✳ JUNE 3, 1992: The search has been suspended for three men from an overturned canoe found in Kachemak Bay Monday.

✳ APRIL 30, 1991: The USCG has suspended its search for two men from the fishing vessel *Berta J* after it sank fifty miles south of Yakutat.

✳ APRIL 22, 1991: The USCG has suspended its search for a German hiker in Glacier Bay National Park.

✳ NOVEMBER 25, 1991: The USCG suspended its search for four people who abandoned their fishing vessel in Bristol Bay, about one hundred miles north of Cold Bay, on Friday. Search efforts covered more than 3,600 square miles in the east Bering Sea.

✳ NOVEMBER 25, 1991: The Coast Guard suspended its search for a man missing in the vicinity of Tongass Narrows, in southeast Alaska, early this afternoon.

The Coast Guard searched for three days, using a helicopter from Air Station Sitka and a forty-one-foot utility boat from Station Ketchikan, without finding sixty-four-year-old Erwin Curell. Curell was planning to make a round trip from Ketchikan to Pennock Island. After returning to Ketchikan, he was to visit his daughter in Portland, Oregon. When he failed to arrive as scheduled, his daughter notified the Alaska state troopers. They found Curell's car parked near the city float in Ketchikan with parking tickets indicating it had been there since Tuesday. Curell had planned to use a skiff on the trip to Pennock Island and a small inflatable on the way back.

The subject of a search might be walrus hunters, kayakers, canoists, jet skiers, campers, Coast Guardsmen and other searchers, hikers, fliers, windsurfers, fishers, crabbers, a grounded ferry, a tugboat, a raft, or a barge. Sometimes the subject is a hoax. Sometimes evidence is as flimsy as a flare or a bit of debris, or a wavering voice unable to give location. Sometimes it is a screaming, incoherent voice, a sound portrait of panic.

More dramatic searches take weeks, or even months. The search for my colleague Kent Roth fills pages but now lies below layers and layers of paper giving reports on other searches. You want to shout, No, don't stop. Find him. Find his plane. His family has obtained tapes from the Federal Aviation Administration and had them digitized. They claim they hear Jeff, the pilot, speaking. This helps them to know where to search. Why wasn't this done before? Why aren't more people, planes, experts, and resources being put into the search? They have only so much time. Already Land Otter Men might have taken them, Kent and his brothers and their friends, or the Spirit of Lituya Bay. Already they might be slaves. Winter is coming. Winter is nearly here. For Franklin in 1826, it had long since come. For Franklin in June 1847, it would never come again.

I remember De Long, of the *Jeannette,* who struggled for years to survive, finally succumbing very close to rescue, and not before, in a final act, throwing his journal behind him to save it from the coming floods. I think of Franklin, who struggled over so many miles, leaving so many clues along the way, but none that yet gives us total resolution. I remember Rasmussen, who found the bones and belongings of Franklin victims on the east coast of Adelaide Peninsula and who spoke to the offspring of those who found the Franklin ships; Rasmussen, who spoke to the last of the shamans, who gave us some of their words, otherwise lost forever. The links continue. There is always hope, or is there? There has to be. Lady Franklin never gave up. Under her direction, McClintock and Hobson found the only known Franklin record, in a cairn that Franklin's men had found from the earlier Ross expedition, which located the Magnetic North Pole.

The Begiches don't forget, nor the Roths. Cairns are

everywhere, with their buried, waiting messages. They need only be found. Clues and omens are everywhere—in our dreams, in the flight of birds, in the bend of the grass. Can we find them in time? Can we read them?

Clouds, water, ashes, wind: The world waits to be read, to be interpreted, reinterpreted, created, and recreated.

Kazantzakis's Saint Francis was offered divination by a caged mouse—a white mouse said to be from Paradise.

For the ancient Chinese, writing was a tool of divination. And for me. I keep reading, writing, marking.

Keep on, you want to shout. Keep on. Don't let him disappear. Don't let them disappear. Don't let any of them disappear. We no longer have shamans but we have radar, we have spy planes, we have satellites, GPS, a technology that can reach to the stars and beyond, one that must be able to see through ice and snow. But it is so large, the place where they might have fallen. God, it is so large. And the snow falls so quickly and so deep. It is so hard to see!

Even if we threw dogs or slaves into the crevasses, it wouldn't be enough. Rotting flesh is no longer enough. The Malaspina Glacier is moving. The Bering Glacier is moving. The Bering Glacier, indeed, is throwing icebergs, huge icebergs, into the gulf; no ship is safe. The tankers are endangered. The black heart of Alaska waits to crack open on an iceberg.

* * *

Often explorers, searching for what existed only in imagination, stumbled—or foundered—upon something else. Stefansson found the cairn on the north tip of Prince Patrick Island containing the message left by McClintock sixty-two years earlier on his search for the Franklin party. And Stefansson's cairn was later found. A letter that the Dutch explorer Willem Barents placed in the fireplace of his house of refuge at Ice Haven on Novaya Zemlya in 1597 was found almost three hundred years later, along with the shoes of his little servant boy.

De Long was found, though dead, his left arm and hand raised out of the snow as if in greeting, his face still wearing lifelike color. He and his frozen men were transported home for heroes' burials.

They were following a map; they were rewriting a map. Incorrect maps led them beyond imagination to what we might say was real; errors guided them. Hence Bering and Chirikov came to southeast Alaska, and Columbus came to what we now call the West Indies. Today we rewrite the map from space; the Milky Way becomes our zero line. Perspective shifts. Scale changes. The horizon moves out, pulling us with it, trying to define it, trying to set it down. Still, no map can be entirely accurate, nor our reading of it assured.

There is a framed original chart from the Cook expedition to Alaska in 1778—Cook's last before he turned south to Hawaii and death at the hand of native Hawaiians. The chart, in pencil, was executed by either Cook or Master William Bligh, for whom Bligh Reef was named—the reef that gashed the *Exxon Valdez* in 1989 and caused such loss. (Retired Juneau professor Wally Olson is quite sure it is Bligh's hand.) It is a working chart of Unalaska Island, out in the Aleutians, made during the summer as Cook and his men headed north to Icy Cape, at the edge of the Frozen Sea.

There, just off the coast of the island, in a faint but elegant hand, this notation:

All this 30′ west of the truth

Position needs always to be reassessed, the coordinates recalculated, our place on earth defined. In Cook's and Bligh's time, "truth" was established when chronometers had been adjusted and all known navigational readings had been coordinated to determine position. That corrected position, at that moment, was "the truth."

Still we are trying to find it. Our stories, our memories, our celebrations and rituals, are the coordinates that hold us in place. Poets defy gravity and physicists argue the bending of time and space. In the meantime, we set the table, call the children home, take our appointed places, perhaps say grace, pass the food in a certain way. Each table where we gather is unique and as vital to those who sit there as a nautical chart is to a sailor.

As Helen, Tom, and Sam grew up, there was in our kitchen one bent stainless steel spoon known as "the spoon." Whoever got to set the table could assign it to a victim. The victim was expected to howl in protest and always did. Now when we say, "Remember the spoon?" a flood of associated memories returns. It is as good as a chronometer, or as a chart of the heavens. It is a mark on the way, just as Franklin's monogrammed silver spoons and forks, abandoned on the fatal ice, are a mark on the way.

AUGUST 20

Today the sound and sight of a flock of bohemian waxwings shaking two mountain ash trees full of bright orange berries. These birds are gypsy fruit-eaters. They appear at random through the winter, their bell-like call a sign of hope. There is something to eat here. We are refuge in the swirling winter storms. Nearly always, the bohemian waxwings return at Thanksgiving, quite often on the very day.

Yesterday a mother bohemian waxwing with two fledglings in a neighbor's cherry tree. Tomorrow, perhaps, the first big storm blowing in from the gulf.

I suddenly remember: In childhood, I once owned a canary. I remember its tremulousness but not its name or how it left me. Did I neglect it? Did it die because I did not love it?

What a trail of beloved animals lies behind me, as I dare to look: There was Little Breeches, my hunter-pony.

She died in comfortable retirement on a farm in Pennsylvania, but in all the years after I rode her and won all those ribbons with her, I never went to see her to say goodbye or thank you. She had taught me much, being a far better performer than I was a rider. There was Sister Agnes, the cat with a big white bib rescued from St. Dominic's Church, where the nuns who taught me catechism wore habits with large white bibs. There was her strange lout of a son, Felix, who turned on faucets; her sweet daughter, Punkin; and the orange cats who had fits. There were the cocker spaniels and the chickens, the Hampshire pigs, and the baby alligator, the turtles, the fish, and the long, long line of pet mice, one buried under a sarcophagus at Bryn Mawr.

There were the gerbils, which traveled to Alaska with us, the hamster, and the many, many rabbits, whose care I so neglected. The rabbits came when Helen, needing positive reinforcement at school, won them as part of a contract. Then there were many rabbits, each different. I was very fond of each of them but did not give them the care I would have liked to. Forgive me, rabbits. There was Boy, who guarded us so fiercely but who was so tender with the children. Once, when by previous arrangement my dear friend Mary Ellen came to our house to change clothes when we were not there, he would not let her in. He would go through windows to get at the mail carrier, the cleaner's delivery person. The morning Martin took him to be put to sleep, I could not go. I said goodbye to him at the door and went to the office, pretending to work. Now he is always waiting at the door. Forgive me, Boy. Forgive me, each animal, for how I failed you. So often, it seems, as I look back, I was in a whiteout.

AUGUST 21

Today is Sam's last day before he leaves to start college —at Reed, in Portland. At least he is not traveling across the country, as he did during the boarding school years, the years when he seemed at times a little boy and my heart was cracking for his farness, for the tears that would push up against the dam of his eyelids but never spill over. That is a journey I am glad is done. We celebrate tonight with a party outdoors, in a glorious burst of clear weather.

Today the yearly supply barges made it into Barrow, at the top of the state. Though ice had threatened arrival, enough open water held. The groceries and modular housing units had arrived. A hundred years ago, it would have been time for the whalers to have left. Read the incantation in the maritime records: "Trapped by ice; crushed in ice; wrecked in autumn gale; stranded and lost in heavy seas."

Today announcement was made of the discovery of a crash site from two years ago. The plane carrying two Tok hunters has been found. It took two years, I remember, to find Ben Iverson's plane; but the discovery of his plane led only to greater questions, questions yet to be answered.

Today the search was suspended for the British tourist miss-ing in Sitka. A Coast Guard helicopter found no traces on Mount Verstovia, where he was thought to have gone hik-ing. The last trace of Peter John Cowley was a credit card charge for passage on a ferry from Wrangell to Sitka on July 10. And then there was the Sitka resident who thought he had given such a person a lift to the Mount Verstovia trailhead. There was nothing certain, nothing but that sig-nature on a charge slip—the precious last words.

"Verstovia" comes from the Russian term *verst*, a unit of distance equal to 0.662 miles, and was given in 1809 by the navigator Ivan Vasiliev. I look for a reference to this early Russian navigator but cannot find one, the name of his captain, his ship—a gap.

Often journals, even if we do find them, don't tell us what we want—or need—to hear. Bartlett would not men-tion suicide. Lorne Knight's journals from Stefansson's first expedition to Wrangel Island were edited by the troubled Harold Noice and became the subject of bitter dispute. Jim Huscroft's journals of Lituya Bay, except for one, have not been found; stories, some undoubtedly apocryphal, contra-dict one another as to what happened to them. Were they thrown by robbers into a fire, or were they simply allowed to be forgotten, to molder away in the rain of the southeast coast? And were the Franklin journals torn into playthings for children and committed that way to the winds? Or did they simply sink with the ships that carried them? How many times have they circled the pole in the slow cauldron of ships and logs and useless charts, wearing down to smaller and smaller pieces?

How many times have we been cheated, or stolen from? I begin to make a list: the time I looked down the stairwell in our house in Oyster Bay to see burglars looking up at me with a flashlight; the time I ran a purse-snatcher to ground in New York; the jewelry stolen from a suitcase left on a bus in New York; the diamond ring stolen by a baby-sitter in Boulder. It then gets more complicated and painful and I give it up. I have been stolen from. I am no longer whole, but I go on. Kent Roth has been stolen from, and certainly his family. The skies and the oceans steal, and we steal from one another's hearts. In the former slave states, a slave was accused of "theft of self" if he or she escaped. Theft of self: a kind of disappearance.

Lady Sarashina, you are one who cheated me. You left me poems and scraps of dreams but not your name, your story, your self. I do not know where you went after ending your book, though it was probably to a temple in the hills where a bell continued to ring long after your ashes had become illegible. I will never hold your last precious words or know what you might have told me. That message might have saved me. It might have given me strength —a cache of energy stashed on the way, able to inspire new hope and commitment.

According to the Eskimo Whaling Commission, the first fall bowhead has been struck by a boat from Kaktovik.

The bowhead, *Balaena mysticetus*, is a large baleen whale found in Arctic waters. Growing as long as sixty-five feet, it usually weighs a ton for every foot of its length. Heavily exploited by commercial whalers between 1848 and about 1915, it is now found chiefly in the Bering, Chukchi, and Beaufort seas and numbers about 7,800: an endangered species. Presently it is hunted only by the Native residents of nine Alaska villages: Gambell, Savoonga, Wales, Kivalina, Point Hope, Wainwright, Barrow, Nuigsut, and Kaktovik. This limited subsistence hunt is tightly controlled on three levels: on the local, through the Alaska Eskimo Whaling Commission, established in 1978; on the national, by the National Marine Fisheries Service; and on the international, through the International Whaling Commission. The goal is to enable the Native people to maintain their ancient relationship with the animal upon which they have always depended and which had been driven close to extinction.

By 1849, the year of the California gold rush, 154 whaling ships had sailed into the icy Arctic waters in a rush of their own. By the next year, there were two hundred. Huge harvests of oil and baleen magnetized the industry as it moved farther to the north and to the east, across the top of Alaska. And as the bowhead was hunted to near extinction, so was the walrus, the lifeblood of the Eskimo people.

AUGUST 26

✳ *Today the Coast Guard, Alaska Air National Guard, and Civil Air Patrol continue searching for a Beechcraft Bonanza missing for nine days.* The plane, piloted by retired Navy captain Franklin Roth, was en route from Kenai to Whitehorse, in the Yukon Territory. The last radio contact with the plane was just east of Gulkana, when the pilot reported some icing on his wings. So far, 13,500 square miles have been covered in the search.

I note the two names, an unlucky convergence. Press on, I want to say. Don't let there be another one.

AUGUST 28

The search continues for the plane missing near Gulkana, in the Glennallen area. Bad weather and fallout from the volcanic eruption of Mount Spurr have impeded the effort, but the Rescue Coordination Center at Elmendorf Air Force Base insists that the search will go on.

Today, in brightening late-summer weather, I walk along the Perseverance Trail, where Jeff Scharff disappeared. I am with my friend Patricia and my chocolate Lab, Kaleb. The salmonberries are at their deepest red. The foliage is poised to turn, the chapter of summer giving way to the chapter of winter. The water rushes through Ebner Falls. I call the dog back when he approaches the edge. The power tears at my heart. Just downstream from where I watch, a slippery fallen tree crosses the tumultuous falls. There is a small rope railing along it. That might be the spot. There are no birds, no messages.

I think about why we walk on such a trail, why we travel, explore. As we walk, I discuss past lives with Patricia. She tells me of hers—as astronomer, as mountain climber, as railroad builder. She says that life is a spiritual journey and that the universe gives us all we need. There can be no disaster, no spiritual disaster. The worst that can happen, even with suicide, is that we have to come back and learn the lesson; it is like having to repeat a class. Finally we move on. But there is always more to move on to. And beyond this galaxy there are many others. We need only trust to the working of the universe, which gives us everything we need.

I remember Rasmussen quoting Igjugarjuk: "No life once given can ever be lost or destroyed."

What disappears only slips from our physical eyesight

beyond a horizon we cannot quite see. Nothing can be lost. The universe knows where we are—and cares. We have only to ask if that is not so. But we forget to ask, or are afraid to ask. I hear this, I know this, but still I search. I can't let go of fear, the force that pushes me to make this map, to put the dark dots down.

RECORD 11

It was the time when children leave. Now the youngest child, about to turn eighteen, had left for college. It was the time of emptiness and foreboding.

Years before, on the morning I was leaving with Helen to take her to her new school in New Hampshire, I said goodbye to Tom at the front door. It was dark and windy. He was on his way out to go duck hunting on the Mendenhall Refuge. I felt drawn to his right cheek, needing to rub it, to kiss it. All day, as I traveled, I thought of his cheek, soft and strangely vulnerable. That night, when I called home from New York, I heard he had been shot, inside that cheek, by another young duck hunter firing a twelve-gauge shotgun. The shot entered his open mouth as he yelled to the other boy to hold his fire, and lodged in the inside skin.

Our party is accounted for. Not exactly together, or intact, but accounted for. I know the phone numbers for each. I go on, alone again with my mate, leaving messages. It is almost winter.

CHAPTER XII

Summer Ends

AUGUST 31

I am trying to pack up the house for the winter, preparing for other people to live in it. It is hard to know what is important to save and what is not—what might make a difference.

When hydrographers are doubtful, they label an island "E.D.," existence doubtful. Sometimes it is not only existence but loss itself that is doubtful.

✳ *In Fairbanks, authorities are trying to identify a skeleton recently found in a burned-out cabin.* There are no clues to that identification. Who might have met such an end, that no one knew or protested that there was a disappearance? A disappearance will be pursued only so far as there is someone who notices, cares, pronounces it and will not let it go.

Today in Barrow the first bowhead of the fall season has been struck, and in Kaktovik a second one.

✳ *Three men from Noorvik are missing from a twenty-foot skiff that capsized on its way home from Kotzebue.* One body has been found. Thirty boats and a hundred people have participated in the search, centering on Hotham Inlet, six miles northeast of Kotzebue.

Tourists continue to come to Juneau—four ships carrying a total of 5,500 passengers today—*but there are no more statements about Walter Shaw, nor are there any posters remaining that declare him to be missing.* Walter Shaw disappears from our consciousness. Walter Shaw disappears again. Only the universe knows where he is.

Sometimes, as in the case of the Fairbanks cabin, the body lies beneath our feet but we do not recognize it. Sometimes we do not know what to search for. At other times we do not know that there is something to search for. Disappearance can be forgotten or not recognized. And what we fear is that—the ultimate disappearance of being forgotten. It was not the fear of Rasmussen's Eskimo companion who could leave behind his wife, discovered frozen to death on the trail, but I begin to see it as my fear. Can written words save? Is ultimate existence dependent on words prodding the memory of those left behind? Do the dead need to be invoked, their names chanted from an ice journal?

SEPTEMBER 1

Today the search for the three missing Noorvik men continues on the Kobuk River. Years ago, I was in Kotzebue at Easter. I was told the story of how a resident, Charlie Rich, had had a battle the night before with spirits on a frozen lake. They had tried to make him turn around and travel toward Noorvik. He fought them all night, and won. He made it home to Kotzebue.

In the Arctic, the spirit world is real. People talk about encounters with spirits and of visions in a matter-of-fact manner. Visions in the sky have been experienced by pilots and by dog mushers. In southeast Alaska too they are not unknown.

In February 1973, crewmen aboard the Alaska state ferry *Malaspina* recorded in the log the following account of a sighting of the *Flying Dutchman* near Ketchikan:

The ship's position when sighting was abeam of Twin Island, Revillagigedo Channel. The time was 0655 hours Pacific Standard time. The weather was clear with unlimited visibility. Wind Northeast 10 knots, temperature 28 degrees, and the barometer pressure was 30.71.

Standing watch on the bridge was Chief Mate Walter Jackinsky and two sailors—one at the helm and one lookout. A huge vessel was seen approximately eight miles dead ahead, broadside and dead in the water. This vessel resembled very much the *Flying Dutchman*. The color was all gray

—similar to vapor or clouds. It was seen distinctly for about ten minutes. It looked so exact, natural and real that when seen through binoculars sailors could be seen moving on board. Within seconds it disappeared into oblivion.

This is the first such sighting to any of these present, all of whom were in full agreement.

A month before, a woman employee on the *Malaspina* had jumped to her death approximately 200 miles south of Ketchikan, or about 190 miles south of the sighting. The *Malaspina* was the ferry that had brought me and Helen and Tom to join Martin in Juneau (Sam had not yet been born). It was early in October. The light over the Inside Passage was silver. In Wrangell, when we stopped, I walked along the streets and saw dahlias. I thought southeast Alaska was a place of silvery light and huge autumn flowers. I did not yet know the country I had entered.

Later, when I heard about the *Flying Dutchman*, I was not surprised. I had been brought up with ghosts. Early one Christmas morning, as my sister and I returned from midnight mass, we encountered a nimbus at the top of our driveway, where the car caught on ice. Unable to break free, we fled from the car and ran to the house, to the lights we understood.

Earlier, as a child, I had heard the story of the ghost that appeared to my grandparents at their house in Walpole, New Hampshire. One summer's night after dinner my grandparents were sitting out on the lawn with my great-aunt, Katherine Parsons, and her husband, John. (It was the house where Louisa May Alcott wrote *Under the Lilacs*, and the lilacs were still there.) Suddenly the phantom of a young woman in white rushed up to them, her feet just above the grass, as if to implore their help, then vanished. The next morning they learned that at that time a young woman had been murdered down by the railroad tracks.

In my horseback-riding youth, I was friends with an Irish groom, Wilkie Collins, who bore the same name as the nineteenth-century author and creator of the first mystery stories, *The Woman in White* and *The Moonstone*. And I was left a moonstone necklace by my great-aunt Margaret Sheffield, a treasure that now lives in our bank vault in Juneau. A translucent band of names and connections held all together. That a face, or a ship, would suddenly appear out of context seemed not at all unusual. It was like one gem in a strand catching fire with light and forcing our attention.

Captain Bartlett, when asked if he believed in ghosts, answered, "Sometimes I do and sometimes I don't. When there's a bad shipwreck I do; especially if the ship disappears." He tells the story of the *Berkeley*, a herring boat out of Labrador, which disappeared with all ninety-seven hands. That night, in three different families, the absent crew members appeared in soaking clothes and then quickly disappeared, forever. In a number of other tales Bartlett tells, a crew member dripping with water appears to a loved one to signal the loss of his ship: The sea is made of mothers' tears. But the worst thing, Bartlett says, is disappearance.

> As a matter of fact in my nearly forty years the most terrible thing I've encountered in all my hard voyages has not been fire or shipwreck, gale or blizzard or starvation. It has been the horrible sense of helpless grief that comes when men sail away and never come back.
>
> If you know your husband or father or brother is dead, you can bear the loss. But if you picture him year in year out dying by inches on some desert island or wandering with lost memory on some distant shore, a bitter anguish haunts you night and day.
>
> From this cause I have seen aged men die; gay young wives grow old and grim; mothers weep their hearts out until the grave relieves their despair; and both sisters and brothers turn cold shoulders to a happy world in the awful thrall of a never-ending hope.

The strangest stories Bartlett tells, however, are of ships found floating with their crews gone: the *Marie Celeste*, off Gibraltar (a child's dress still in a sewing machine); a schooner from Cadiz, off Newfoundland (a fire burning in the galley, a pot of soup overturned); and the Norwegian sealer *Isstjernen*, found drifting off Newfoundland (the table set, the lamps lighted).

SEPTEMBER 2

The search continues along the Kobuk River for the three missing men from Noorvik. It is reported that hopes are dwindling, because the men were not wearing survival suits.

✳ *Near Haines, north of Juneau, a sixteen-year-old deckhand has drowned in a boating accident.* When the fishing boat he was working on capsized, he was trapped inside. The twenty-year-old skipper escaped. The accident occurred at Seduction Point, fifteen miles south of Haines, in thirty-knot winds and four-foot seas. He was only sixteen. The hair had barely begun to grow on his face.

It is reported that the skeleton found in the burned cabin in Fairbanks is that of a woman in her twenties. Forensic medicine is now being used to identify a person never known to have disappeared, perhaps, except by those who caused her disappearance.

Forensic medicine helps us to see in a new way: to learn that what we look at can be different from what we think. A body, even that of an infant, is a map, a record of long journeyings and discovery, an accumulation of coordinates. The scars, the lines, the contours, the indentations and rises, the protruding veins and discolorations of freckle, birthmark, and bruise, are all symbols on the map of a life.

And that life, once given, can never be lost or destroyed. A name is a map. And a name, once given, can never be lost or destroyed. But no map can give us an accurate reading, and no means of navigation can assure us of where we are.

SEPTEMBER 3

After a long silence in the press, the case of Kent Roth comes back, for the coroner's jury. Four of the five men aboard the missing plane have been declared presumed dead. Gayle Roth, wife of the pilot, Jeff, asked that her husband not be included in the proceedings. She believes that her husband is still alive and protests that she will wait.

"Somehow," she is reported as saying, "I feel they're going to make it out on their own. Each of the five families has to do what they have to do to continue their families. To me, the most comfortable thing is to continue to wait. And pray."

Air Force Lieutenant Colonel Mike Callahan, in charge of the rescue efforts, told jurors that if the men had survived the crash, they could have lived up to five days before succumbing to hypothermia.

Another Roth brother, Jason, thirty-six, had also been on the fishing trip to Yakutat but had left six hours earlier in his own plane. When the coroner asked him what he thought had happened, Jason Roth answered, "I think they caught ice and it brought them down."

Gayle Roth, certain that the plane landed on either the

Malaspina or the Bering Glacier, hoped that the recent eruption of Mount Spurr would coat the glaciers with gray volcanic ash and that rain, washing the plane, would expose it against the gray of the ice. She said she will keep looking for her husband—forever, if that's what it takes. "Till he comes home," she said.

SEPTEMBER 4

Wavering autumnal sun works its way through the leaves. Clouds hug the mountains. I continue to make and remake piles—what to save, what to give away, what to abandon. There are old calendars, clips, manuscripts, bank accounts, pay stubs, report cards, thank-you cards, birthday cards. Yesterday, Helen's birthday; tomorrow, our anniversary; two days later, Sam's birthday.

I think about their births, all three in the early morning. For Helen, born shortly after eight, and Tom, born shortly after four—both in Denver—I heard birds singing. Sam, at 4:21, was born in Juneau in a room without a window.

In Anchorage, Gayle Roth, determined not to be a widow, settles into another day. I think of Lady Franklin, who also never gave up, not even when the grim truth was known. Traveling to Sitka in 1870, when she was seventy-eight, she still hoped to find traces, some sort of document that would tell more of the story. And how glad she was to be able to share copies of McClintock's book recounting the adventures of the *Fox*.

Sometimes, as with the Franklin tragedy, search is necessary to learn what we would not have learned if we had not been searching. Sometimes the story is not meant to be known.

In Fairbanks, anthropologists have now concluded that the woman whose skeleton was found was between twenty-nine and thirty-four when she was shot. She was five feet, four inches tall. She was Caucasian or possibly part Alaska Native and had had extensive dental work done. The house had most recently been lived in by the absent owner's son, who died in 1988. After his death, neighbors had complained about his acquaintances moving in and causing problems. When the owner traveled to Fairbanks to investigate, he found his son's valuables gone.

Sometimes great waves come out of the sea, and sometimes the earth contorts itself as it moves. Sometimes people disappear in such times of natural disaster, as in Lituya Bay. Sometimes they simply disappear. Sometimes they are loved and remembered and searched for, for as long as those who love them live. Sometimes they are forgotten. Sometimes there is no one to come forward and identify their bones, the map they leave behind.

It was twenty-one years ago today—September 4, 1971—that an Alaska Airlines Boeing 727 jetliner en route from Yakutat to Juneau crashed on a mountainside in the Chilkat

Range eighteen miles west of Juneau, killing all 111 on board. At the time, it was the worst air disaster to have occurred in the United States.

Alaska Airlines Flight 1866 had originated in Anchorage, with stops in Cordova and Yakutat. It was making its approach to the Juneau airport in rain and fog when it slammed into the 2,500-foot level of the mountain range at a site one mile east of Teardrop Lake. The flight crew, following a directional system, thought they had cleared the mountain range, but the plane was actually nine miles to the west of where they thought it was, on the wrong side of the wall of mountains. Flight 1866 was, indeed, nine miles west of the truth—the position as calculated.

Certain changes occurred. The Juneau airport gained an instrument landing system to supplement the directional system, which continues to be used. Four passengers had been students at Mt. Edgecumbe High School in Sitka, operated then by the Bureau of Indian Affairs to provide secondary education to Alaska Natives who did not have high schools in their home towns. In 1976, the Molly Hootch case (now officially titled *Tobeluk* v. *Raynolds)* mandated a high school in every village in Alaska that has an elementary school and that wants one. But for those on the flight from Yakutat that day, the legal decision and the new navigational system came too late; there could be no correction.

Today I happen to read in the obituaries a notice of the death of a friend and former colleague, the Tlingit artist Robert James "Jim" Schoppert, who died in Ojai, California, at age forty-five, no reason given. Once he worked with me in a statewide prison education program. When we first came to Juneau and bought our house, twenty-one years ago, he was looking for work. We hired him to rebuild part of our foundation. He was an accomplished sculptor and printmaker.

My last conversation with Jim was high in the air in an Alaska Airlines 737 from Anchorage to Juneau. We traveled together over the Bering and Malaspina glaciers, over Yakutat, over Lituya Bay, over the Chilkats, over the crash site of Alaska Airlines Flight 1866 and the crooked dog-leg course into Juneau. Then we parted, and he went out of my life.

I never got any of Jim's artwork, but we have his foundation. It is on the north side, the side away from the sun, the side that takes the cold, the side where our bed is. In the woods, sometimes moss grows on the north side; if not the north, at least one side.

There are certain compass plants, as well. In the tundra, male catkins, or pussywillows, grow red with spring pollen on the south side. If you are observant and know the ways of plants, sometimes you can find your way. Sometimes.

✳ *A body has been found by fishermen at Alitak Bay, in the southwest corner of Kodiak Island.* It is thought to be that of Dennis Welsch, twenty-three, of Wisconsin. Welsch and a companion have been missing since a halibut opening on June 9. Their partially submerged skiff was found earlier.

This was the day when Vitus Bering and his crew met a small band of Aleuts in the Shumagin Islands in 1741—the first contact between Europeans and Native Alaskans. On either side there was, apparently, some thought of a spiritual connection. According to Steller, Bering's naturalist,

> When they were still half a verst away, the two men in the boats, while paddling steadily, began to deliver a long, uninterrupted oration to us in a high-pitched voice, not a word of which any of our interpreters could understand. We took it for either a prayer or a conjuration, the incantation of shamans or a ceremony welcoming us as friends, since both customs are in use on Kamchatka and in the Kurile Islands.

Soon, however, fear and misunderstanding took over. This moment of first contact ended, prophetically, with Bering's men firing muskets over the heads of the Natives to get them to drop the line from the longboat they had taken hold of. A violent storm followed. The Europeans were happy to be on board, while, as Steller comments,

"Our Americans, on the other hand, lit a fire on shore and made us think this night about what had happened."

Igjugarjuk and Najagneq are long since gone, as are the famous shamans of southeast Alaska. Their words of connectedness are gone, as is their faith that nothing of substance separates the worlds of the visible and the invisible. The rod of power—the paraphernalia of the shaman—is broken, or cast aside and lost. Separation leads to the desperate attempts for substitution: alcohol, drugs, suicide. To walk through the cemetery at Kotzebue or Angoon and read the recent dates of death will grip your heart, and in the spring it is worst. June is the peak month for suicides in the Yukon-Kuskokwim basin.

John Active, a Yupik Eskimo writer who lives in Bethel, has commented in the *Anchorage Daily News* on what he views as the extermination of his people—not a direct one, such as the Holocaust, but an indirect one. Yupiks, as he states, are "spiritual by being aware and conscious of everything around us: animals, plants and the environment. We are part of them, and they are part of us. Laws that interfere with that fragile relationship are like cancers. They start by eating just a little of us but end by consuming us completely."

The magnetic pole moves, but we do not know how to follow. We have lost the geomancer's compass, our connection with the pole of harmony. Having destroyed the shaman, we now go seeking him; not finding him, we attempt to recreate him in ourselves. In our non-Native living rooms we court angels and animal totems. We rattle. We drum. We enter a trance state. We journey. We cleanse ourselves. We attempt to reconnect with indigenous and tribal knowledge. We try, indeed, to retribalize. We light the smudge pot and wave the eagle feathers, which we are not allowed to possess but do. We go on spirit quests, then are surprised where they lead us—back to ourselves and a new view of where it is that we stand.

I have done this. Once I went on a spirit quest, in the Juneau living room of my friend Judi, a student of Felicitas Goodman. Judi had us assume one of the ancient postures described by Goodman as connected with specific spirit guides. As she beat her drum, the six of us participating went quietly into different experiences, which we later recounted, for each other and for the record that Judi is keeping for Goodman. I had connected with Land Otter, had become Land Otter. I had felt the fur growing up along my arms and over my body. I had gone into the water, a river. I had swum in fear of people in boats, people on shore. I was happy to climb out on the bank and play in the sun. No experience had ever been more vivid. Later Judi told us that the particular posture she had chosen evoked a spirit quest, and that spirit quests usually involve a sensation of descent, such as under water.

Twenty-four hours later Kaleb, my dog, and I met a land otter on the beach. The land otter lured Kaleb into the water, then led him farther and farther from shore. I screamed for him to come back; finally, in a state of extreme excitement, he did. Kaleb and I had crossed over a boundary. He trembled for hours afterward. Judi told me later my experience was not unexpected: One usually meets the spirit animal physically within one day of the quest.

Autumn fogs continue to rise and fall, with temperatures dropping. The remaining flowers bend deeper. In some gardens, the foxglove stalks are now almost parallel with the ground, close to the voice of the cold. Don't listen, I want to say. Come back! Don't follow down those dark and dangerous cellar steps.

I do not remember, when I was young, such dread of the coming winter. I do not remember such profound sadness at the fate of last flowers. I married at this time.

Indeed, today is our anniversary—our twenty-eighth. We do not celebrate or take much notice. It was a golden day—September 5, 1964, in Oyster Bay. The reception was held under a large yellow and white marquee set up on my parents' place, just beyond the garden. My bridesmaids wore golden yellow dresses. The sun was still shining as Martin and I, in our going-away clothes, walked out the front door to the cheers of family and friends, got in our new car, and headed west, following the sun. We were going to Colorado, to the university in Boulder. We did not know, of course, just how far. Today, I calculate, we have already had twice as long as Kent and Loretta Roth had;

they would have celebrated their fourteenth anniversary three days after the plane dropped from contact.

I look into the west garden. It is my only garden—a raised flowerbed running between our yellow house and the sidewalk on C Street. When we first arrived, it was filled with nasturtiums. Now it holds a yellow globeflower my friend Mary Ellen gave me, strong daylilies and tiger lilies that Martin planted, and white stones brought by my friend Mary from Sheep Creek Valley, a valley threatened with extinction by a proposed mining operation. My garden faces west, catching the last of the sun. During the nights of the summer solstice—if there is sun—that rare and intoxicating light pours down the throats of the yellow and orange lilies until they, and the sky, close. Once, during such a time, while waiting for Martin to get back from the "Spirit of Adventure" race, I wrote an erotic poem full of these lilies. But Martin came home sick, a medical emergency. The race was lost. The lilies withered and dropped their heads. We slid again into winter.

I see no paired butterflies now over the grass in the west garden. We have few butterflies. But there are many grasses, grown wild and brown, vying with the stalks of the dead lilies. They hurt me. I grow older. Already I have been married twenty-eight years. I have seen my children grow up and away. I have left homes, jobs, communities, and books behind me, as well as many friends scattered across the country. Still I do not know the trail—if I can go forward, or if I have left enough marks along the way to be found, and rescued.

SEPTEMBER 6

It is revealed today that radioactive waste was buried thirty years ago at the former Chariot Site near Point Hope, on the northwest coast, just south of Cook's farthest reach. The waste pit, containing fifteen thousand pounds of contaminated material, is buried at a depth of four feet. The Chariot Site was designed for experiments leading to Project Chariot, which was to have blasted a port at Cape Thompson with nuclear bombs. Although twenty-six miles from Point Hope, the site is within a major hunting and fishing area for Point Hope and Kivalina. It had been forgotten until a researcher working on the subject of nuclear contamination in Siberia obtained documents under the Freedom of Information Act. No fences or warning signs mark the area. It had disappeared. No one seemed to remember it was there, or what it might contain.

Today, in the newspaper, the family of the pilot missing in the Gulkana-Glennallen area runs an ad:

A Special Thank You from the family and friends of Capt. Franklin H. Roth, Ret. USN, and Col. Richard L. Johnson, Ret. Army.

We want to thank the Rescue Coordination Center, Civil Air Patrol, State Troopers, National Guard, Park Service, volunteers and everyone else involved, for your continuing efforts to locate them and their aircraft, a Beechcraft Bonanza, lost in the Glennallen area.

Here are families not ready to give up. A plane is very small, and the mountains and the spaces among the mountains are very large. There are huge areas not yet explored, where no human foot has fallen and no human words have been heard in the silence of the snow.

Ten years ago today, in the tiny town of Craig, on Prince of Wales Island, in the southern part of southeast Alaska, eight people were killed on board the purse-seiner *Investor*. The victims included the pregnant wife and two young children of the skipper. After a decade of intense study and debate, two grand jury investigations, two trials, and $3 million in legal fees, it is still not known who committed the murders and burned the boat with its gruesome cargo. Evidence is missing, a killer or killers lost—and unlikely ever to be found.

When I was very young, my cousin Daphne, a young woman, was murdered. I remember my grandmother, screaming down the hill from her house to ours, "Daphne has been murdered! Daphne has been murdered!" Her father, very wealthy, spent a great deal of money on searching for her killer and always maintained that he knew who it was, but nothing could ever be proved. Daphne and her father and mother are gone, the murderer disappeared, the case long since abandoned, like countless other cases.

After twenty-four hours, I remember being told, the trail is cold. It is extremely hard to apprehend a murderer after that, no matter what resources are brought to bear.

Disappearance. Search. Discovery. Disappearance. The cycle etches itself across the Arctic and the subarctic. It is a natural cycle, and one that all of us are heir to, as individuals and as members of religions, beliefs, nations, and waves of life. Shamanism, Christianity, Islam, Buddhism, Hinduism—all will pass, changing into other forms. Our priests, like the shamans, will disappear. Our tribes will disappear. The tracks we leave will disappear. Snow will fall, crevasses close, glaciers move closer to the sea. The ice floes will lock and pull apart, then crush what comes between them, and the clockwise flow around the pole will continue, grinding and scraping in its pure and impartial way. All will be crushed into elemental units. All the books, all the maps, all the charts, the marks—all will swirl in the dust of stars.

SEPTEMBER 8

Thick fog this morning, and the furnace at work, though yesterday, while walking Kaleb, I saw sweet peas and roses.

Yesterday I also made fireweed honey with the last of

the fireweed and clover blossoms I could find. Martin helped me in the near dark of the evening. We searched first by the lake fronting the Mendenhall Glacier. The recipe calls for eighteen fireweed blossoms, eighteen red clover blossoms, and thirty white clover blossoms. It is called "homesteader's honey" and is made by adding the blossoms to a boiling mixture of water, sugar, and alum. It is an alchemy that substitutes for the work of the too-rare Alaska bee. The blossoms seem to explode as I drop them into the boiling mixture, and the scent of late summer rushes into and out of the kitchen, a ghost.

Robins, some speckled with youth, are busy in the berry bushes on their way south. Robins are birds of good fortune, as are sparrows and wrens, especially if seen from the right.

Soon the last tour ships will pass through. The last page of summer will have turned, and color will have disappeared.

Agencies, state and federal, have begun the argument as to who is responsible for the nuclear waste dump near Point Hope. It is not known yet just which isotopes are buried. Nobody can remember. Records are missing, lost.

Contact with white people used to bring more immediately recognizable devastation—alcoholism, measles, influenza, venereal disease, smallpox. The results now, though equally devastating, come in a subtler manner—changed diet, leading to diabetes; radioactive pollutants, leading to cancer; divisiveness within the corporation, leading to alienation. Sometimes there is a gap of years before the effect is known; the trail is hard to pick up.

SEPTEMBER 9

✳ *Alaska state troopers report that an Anchorage hunter has found what appears to be a human skull in the Pass Creek Trail area near Cantwell.*

About a week after Sam was born, all five of us went on a special trip the Alaska ferry system provided to Glacier Bay National Park. When we left home under dark clouds, we feared we might not see anything—and it was the first time for each of us to the fabled land of glaciers forty miles northwest of Juneau. As we went through Icy Strait, however, the sky cleared. By the time we entered Muir Inlet, the eastern arm of the bay, the sun was shining. We traveled past the petrified forest and the McBride Glacier to the Riggs Glacier and beyond, as far as it was possible to go, to the Muir Glacier.

Two hundred years before, when George Vancouver sailed by, naming much in our area, the entire bay was sealed in ice. Only a hundred years before, in 1879, had John Muir penetrated part of it; vast reaches were still encased, and the Hoonah Tlingits told him it was filled with evil spirits, including Kooshdaka.

Sam slept peacefully. In front of the Riggs Glacier, the crew blew the ship's horn, and a sheet of deep blue ice broke off, or calved. Helen, nine, and Tom, six, were unimpressed; they had expected the whole face to break away; and no whales showed themselves that day. But they were happy with the sunshine and the hamburgers —and the ketchup.

CHAPTER XIII

A Walk into the Wild

SEPTEMBER 10

We approach the autumn equinox, the time of winds, storms, and high tides. The southbound waterfowl fly against clouds and early moons. Once, with my friend Jo visiting from Fairbanks, I stood outside our house one early morning and watched geese flying across a rainbow.

It is the last chance to pick blueberries from the wet, cold bushes, their leaves now spotted like the breasts of young robins making their first trip down the coast.

Now is the time for weathergrams, created by Lloyd J. Reynolds, a former calligrapher and professor at Reed College, and designed for the Northwest. Weathergrams are short haiku-like messages written on strips of biodegradable paper and hung with biodegradable material on trees. They are meant to be placed along paths, in parks, or by windows where they will be seen and to weather away with the elements. They might last, perhaps, from autumn equinox to vernal equinox.

I had done them with young writers all over the state. In the papers I now sort, I find many examples. Sam, when he was very young, drew a child's sun. It shines now as I pull it out of a box of scraps.

The disappearance of Alaska's dinosaurs surfaces and subsides as a point of interest. The International Conference on Arctic Margins has just completed a meeting on the subject. It is thought now that the hadrosaurs that inhabited the North Slope stayed year-round and did not migrate, as was previously postulated.

＊ *Today state troopers released information on a dead hiker whose body was found by hunters in a remote area southwest of Fairbanks.* The man, whose identity is still not known, left notes on the back page of a paperback book. The book, *Tanaina Plantlore*, is about the Athabaskan use of local plants for food and medicine. The notes indicate that the man died in July, 113 days after starting a trek down the Stampede Trail, which leads into Denali National Park. The body was found in an abandoned bus that has been used through the years by hunters seeking shelter. The bus is about seven miles from a ranger station inside the park. The notes indicate that the man, who was injured, survived on berries and game. At one point he shot a moose, which he quickly regretted when the meat turned maggoty.

A note was attached to the outside of the bus:

> SOS. I need your help. I am injured, near death, and too weak to hike out of here.
>
> I am all alone, this is no joke. In the name of God, please remain to save me. I am out collecting berries close by and shall return this evening. Thank you. August?

The body was found on September 6.

Another note, inside a camera case, was found: "I have had a happy life and thank the Lord. Goodbye and may God bless all!"

The body has been taken to the crime laboratory in Anchorage for identification. *There it will lie near the remains of the woman found in the burned-out cabin in Fairbanks and the skull found at Cantwell.*

SEPTEMBER 11

This morning, loud chatterings of robins under a dark gray sky.

＊ *Two boats are reported overdue after the halibut opening, one from Sitka, one from Yakutat.*

The weather report predicts frost for the first time tonight. The robins have far to travel, and how much farther the hummingbirds, whimsically said to make their way north to Alaska each spring on the wings of the sandhill cranes.

Frost, rime, glaze, sleet, graupel, snow: how many forms it takes, falling endlessly out of the northern skies. The simplest snow crystals fall in the highest latitudes. They are falling now, the simple six-sided crystals of ice, over the lost and the disappeared, over those we have searched for and those we have not.

The first Westerner to record the shape of the snow-flake was Olaus Magnus, archbishop of Uppsala, Sweden, in 1550. The first Westerner to note the hexagonal nature of snow crystals was the astronomer Johannes Kepler, in 1610. But in China, the amazing discovery had long since been made. Han Ying, a scholar of the second century B.C., wrote in a poem that most flowers have five petals but only snow crystals have six.

I wonder what the six-sided nature of the snow crystals means: Is it related to the hexagram of the *I Ching?* There is the hexagram of the wasp's cell in its hive; the hexachord; the hexameter; the hexaemeron, or the six days of the Creation. Perhaps it is that—each flake is a representation of the Creation, just as each cell is a representation of the body. If it is so, then flowers, which I love beyond all the beautiful things of earth, are less highly evolved than snow, which I fear. But perhaps that is why they are beautiful: They are striving for perfection.

As the rain clears, fresh snow is visible on all the peaks.

How can we divine meaning from a six-sided storm that disguises and hides a landscape?

Later in the day, the fishing boats from Sitka and Yakutat are still overdue, and Coast Guard searches are under way.

Squalls of heavy rain are separated by bursts of sunshine. The physics of the air is volatile and hungry, the flight of robins fragile and important. May no single bird drop out of formation and be lost along the way. May there be no variations to alter the compass in their hearts.

State troopers have not been able to identify the remains of the hiker found dead in his sleeping bag in the converted bus on Stampede Trail. He signed a name to the SOS note. Film found in his camera will be developed. Officials in other states have been notified, but no local missing-persons reports appear to be relevant.

In Point Hope, villagers have been assured by the Alaska Department of Environmental Conservation that preliminary tests in the Project Chariot area show no danger to inhabitants. More testing, at a deeper level, is planned. An inch of snow has fallen in the area.

Project Chariot, if it had been completed, would have blasted the earth with nuclear power, altering the terrain, altering the map.

To the south and east, at Denali National Park, in Alaska's heart, five inches of snow have fallen. The climbing season is over. The mountain is alone with its victims.

I decide to visit the grave of Walter Harper and his wife in the Evergreen Cemetery, near my house. It is a silvery late afternoon, heavy cold rain interspersed with light. As I walk onto the soggy grass of the cemetery, the rain holds back, a burst of light crosses the south face of Mount Juneau, and part of a rainbow arcs beyond the large white wooden cross at the head of the burying ground. The berries of the mountain ash trees, so favored by the migrating birds, burn vermilion. I look for the grave but cannot find it. I see many familiar names and the names of friends. I come across "Rusty," with the inscription "Where all children are, 1966–77." It is Rusty Dursma, who died on Mount Juneau when he fell into a crevice on a September afternoon not unlike this. I give up on the Harpers and leave the cemetery. I wonder who has the map of the graves. Perhaps a city employee. Perhaps no one. Who can tell, after years or decades, who is buried where? And when there is no one left who cares, what then? What are these cairns we call graves, with these maps called bodies folded and folded in the earth? Who are we hoping will find them and learn their secret? And what if the secret has been buried another ten feet true north?

SEPTEMBER 12

The shower of migrating birds continues, the robins joined now by sparrows and warblers. They sweep past the windows, shake the crabapple and the mountain ash trees, and fill the gray morning with song. New snow is almost halfway down the mountains.

This was the day when nine whalers were "caught in the ice and abandoned" off Barrow in 1876.

The Coast Guard is expanding its search for the two halibut vessels still missing. According to reports, the weather is worsening. The names of those on board have been broadcast.

The Alaska Aviation Heritage Museum in Anchorage has announced the creation of a memorial fund for a plaque and a garden to honor all aviators who have crashed and remain missing. I like to think they have simply flown out of the sky. Once I had a friend in Juneau whose lover went this way. Long ago, a departing soul was seen as a bird fleeing earth.

SEPTEMBER 13

This morning, no birds and the first frost. In just a day they have left—the robins, the sparrows, and the warblers —barely ahead of the cold. I wonder how far to the south they have gotten—Admiralty Island? Sitka? And what is their route? How many will be lost along the way? There is no "Spirit of Adventure" race for them, only a race against time, against weather.

As late as the eighteenth century, Gilbert White, the English naturalist, believed in the hibernation of swallows, even in the possibility that swallows hibernated in the banks of pools and rivers.

In Fairbanks, volunteers at the Alaska Bird Observatory band and study songbirds in an effort to learn more about the life history of these birds in central Alaska. More than half of the songbirds in Alaska migrate every winter. Two of the birds examined and banded by the observatory this year were alder flycatchers, which breed in Alaska and fly more than ten thousand miles to winter in southeast Peru. Observatory volunteers have banded three thousand birds this year.

In one of our first winters here we found a bohemian waxwing lying exhausted in our yard after a storm. We took it in, put it in a cage, and fed it mountain ash berries, which I had the neighborhood children collect. We called it Beauty Bird. After about two weeks, when a flock of its own appeared, we opened a window and then the cage. The bird hesitated in my hand for a moment, then thrust out with an enormous surge to meet its kind, singing like bells in the steeples of nearby trees.

Once, looking out that same window in the small room at the back (north) end of the house, I experienced communication with a mountain ash. It shook all over with light, and that light was somehow connected with me. Beyond anything, the experience taught me the limitation of language, the prison of the literate mind. The tree, growing across the alley in the corner of the Svobodnys' back yard, leaning over the McLeods' back yard, is much larger now. And the little room has gone from serving as my study to being Sam's first bedroom (the only one he ever had to himself) and on to Martin's study. It now contains, among other things, a six-foot stack of tax boxes, a three-foot stack of insurance papers, and Ignatious, Sam's deepwater mud turtle, to which I feed waxworms from my hand.

The search continues for the Mary May *from Sitka and the* Sea Breeze *from Yakutat, with a total of five men aboard.* Why do these fishing boats have such maddening names? Two aircraft are searching for each boat. Because of debris that has been found, the search areas have been expanded. A raft has been found forty miles north of Sitka and a float with the name *Mary May* several miles to the south. Debris has also been found northwest of Yakutat, but it is not known whether there is a connection with the missing troller. No decision has been made as to how long the search will be continued.

In Point Hope, state and federal government officials continue to maintain that there is no danger from the forgotten nuclear waste dump site. A member of the North Slope Borough health board is quoted: "We've lost faith in the federal and state governments. They used us. How are we going to get that faith again?"

They probably will not. There was very little to begin

with. After the whalers, the walrus killers, the missionaries, the diseases, the corporations, it is surprising there is any.

In Juneau, the Yax Te totem pole at the Auke Recreational Area has been vandalized. During the night someone dowsed the forty-foot pole with fuel and set it on fire. The bottom twelve feet have been damaged, the first four feet heavily so. The pole was created in 1941 by the Hoonah Tlingit carver Frank St. Clair under the auspices of the Civilian Conservation Corps.

By coincidence, the Sunday *Anchorage Daily News* carries a long front-page story on the fate of totem poles in southeast Alaska. Last year, two poles, unknown before, were found in the woods near Klawock, on Prince of Wales Island, in the southernmost part of the state. Experts estimate they were carved no later than the 1890s, though extensive testing will have to be done to determine their age. Recent vandalism of gravesites in the nearby abandoned village of Tuxekan makes authorities nervous. The newly found poles could face a similar fate. The city of Klawock plans to retrieve and preserve the poles.

But the Tlingits carved their stories in wood. They were not afraid to set their stories high and naked to the elements. They were not concerned with saving what they created, though endless controversy now surrounds the saving and ownership of Native artifacts. Many have been stolen.

If Li Po had been a carver instead of a poet, he would

have floated his pieces on rivers. But I save and pack away and now am at a loss. How do I move forward when my boxes are so many and so heavy? How can I say one letter, one piece of children's artwork, one postcard from the dead, is more valuable than another?

SEPTEMBER 14

The Coast Guard has suspended the search for the Mary May *and the* Sea Breeze. On board the *Mary May* were Jeff Anderson, the owner, and crewman Robert Enlowe, both of Sitka. On board the *Sea Breeze* were Walter Prichard, skipper, of Yakutat and deckhands Jay Mattila and Dave Harris, hometowns unknown. Be kind to them, Land Otter People. They went in search of halibut and never meant to lose themselves. They will not understand your shadowy kingdom and will wait to be rescued.

It is the day when the New Bedford whaling fleet was abandoned in 1871, off Point Belcher in the pack ice of an unusually early and severe winter. Approximately twelve hundred men (and a handful of women and children) escaped in open boats to Icy Cape, where seven whalers that had made it through the early ice picked them up and carried them to Honolulu. The New Bedford fleet never recovered.

It is the day when Louise Boyd, one of the last explorers of the high latitudes, died, in 1972. She had asked that her ashes be scattered over Miss Boyd Land, at the head of

Ice Fjord in Greenland—the area she had discovered and mapped. Permits and other obstacles were too great, however. Her friend Dr. Walter Wood arranged instead to have her ashes taken to the last Arctic land she had visited, Alaska. By arrangement with the Naval Arctic Research Laboratory, her ashes were dropped over the Arctic Ocean one hundred miles north of Point Barrow, perhaps where the two U.S. Fish and Wildlife Service polar bear biologists vanished in 1990. Her ashes have long since been carried to Greenland, and some, no doubt, have found their way into the very contours she sought, in the silence of Ice Fjord. There they have fallen into patterns that might be divined, have separated and re-formed.

Again this morning, a bright and silent sky after another frost. Yesterday I saw few birds—three sparrows in mid-afternoon, one sparrow a little later, and two crows. No robins. No ravens. No gulls. This morning, so far, no birds.

At the crime lab in Anchorage, there is still no identification of the hiker who died on the Stampede Trail. But a photograph he took of himself—an emaciated white man in his mid-twenties to thirties—has been developed from his roll of film. A person who says he may have given the hiker a ride to the trail early in May has come forward. The motorist says the hitchhiker wanted to live off the land for a while and had plans to rejoin his family for Thanksgiving. He named the state the hiker said he was from, but that information has not been released. How can it be that he has still not been claimed, not been searched for? Surely he was someone's son, brother, friend. Surely someone has thought of, and missed, that face and found it one worthy to be seen again. If he had a family to join at Thanksgiving, surely someone is concerned about him; but then, he might have convinced them not to worry until then. He might have told them there was no way he could reach them. The autopsy reveals that the man starved to death.

At the forgotten nuclear waste dump site near Point Hope, radioactive readings have been registered, and those taking the readings have pulled back in order to obtain protective clothing.

Last evening, just before dark, I visited the cemetery again in search of Walter Harper's grave. With directions from a friend, I was successful. The Harpers are buried under a large flat tombstone well marked with a border of plants, just down the path from the graves of Joseph Juneau and Richard Harris, the founders of Juneau. Unfortunately, in spite of a flashlight, I could barely make out the letters, well weathered and rubbed. I decided to return in the morning, with a broom, paper, and crayons to make a rubbing—an act that will further erode the markings but the only way I know to read what is there. It seems increasingly important as rain and wind are forecast for the next several days, and we now move inexorably into the storms of winter.

It is cold at the cemetery, though I do hear some songbirds. And, of course, the flat tombstone is colder. I kneel on it and do a rubbing with continuous-feed computer paper and a bright green crayon. The bumpy chartreuse results read:

Here lie the bodies of
Walter Harper
and
Frances Wells his wife
drowned on the *Princess Sophia*
25th Oct. 1918
May light perpetual shine upon them
"They were lovely and pleasant in their lives
and in death they were not devided [sic]." II Samuel 1:23

I look up the biblical reference: "Saul and Jonathan were lovely and pleasant in their lives, and in their death they were not divided: they were swifter than eagles, they were stronger than lions."

Books tell me that Saul was the first king of Israel and Jonathan his son. I am sorry that this is all that is said for the Harpers—Walter, who was the first man to climb McKinley and who was on his way to a career as a medical doctor serving his Athabaskan people on the Yukon, and Frances, a nurse, who was on her way to Red Cross work. I am sorry that even these few words are worn away and barely legible. I am sorry that another winter will soon cover them with rain and ice and snow. I sweep off the tombstone with an old broom and leave.

When the *Princess Sophia* slipped off Vanderbilt Reef in the late afternoon of October 25, 1918, it was snowing so hard there was very little visibility. Rescue boats standing by, including the *King & Winge*, had to take refuge where they could. The next day, as the grim task of finding bodies began, more than two feet of snow lay on the beaches where some of the bodies came ashore. About 180 of the bodies were recovered within a week; more than 80 remained caught in the ship, to be found later by divers. Other bodies were washed far from the site and were not retrieved until late in the following summer. Some were never found. Some could not be identified. Some were never claimed. The tragedy, the worst in the Northwest's maritime history, was completely unnecessary. Before the storm struck, all on board could have been removed to waiting ships, but the captain, citing lack of insurance, refused escape when it was possible.

The little schooner *King & Winge* was the first ship to recover a body the next day. She was the ship that had rescued the survivors of the *Karluk* on Wrangel Island four years before, on September 7, 1914. That had been on her maiden voyage. She had been commissioned as a halibut boat but, having missed the halibut season that year, was leased to a trader as a walrus hunter. She had been christened in Seattle on the morning of March 18, 1914, the same day and time that Captain Bartlett and Kataktovik were setting out from Wrangel Island to find help for the stranded party.

The trader who commissioned her was Olaf Swenson. During the previous season, his ship, the *Belvedere*, had been wrecked in the ice along with the *Karluk* and the *Elvira*, a whaler captained by E. T. Pedersen. Both Swenson and Pedersen escaped overland, to Fairbanks, then found their way down the coast to new ships—Pedersen to the *Herman*, which carried Bartlett from the Siberian coast to St. Michael's, and Swenson to the *King & Winge*.

Three captains lose their ships in the polar ice one season and escape overland. Two assist in the rescue of the third.

Swenson is credited with discovering gold in Siberia in 1905. That discovery undoubtedly brought forth the four prospectors Captain Bartlett encountered in 1914.

If you could project every line of latitude and every line of longitude, you would have 64,440 points of intersection; and at each pole, all meridians meet, all directions are one.

Perhaps coincidence is only another name for geophysical intersection; and when we leave behind the map of lines, we also leave behind the concept of intersection. Things can't "coincide" if they are one. The place called disappearance can't be mapped, because nothing there is separate, lost, or less. Nothing there is in degrees or angles, or either near or far away. I begin to see the map of disappearance as a pure and necessary blankness, something similar to what I saw from the cockpit of the British Airways 747 when flying over the polar ice cap: an expanse of brilliant white with absolutely no marks—the place we go when we are ready, or forced, to throw down language and measurement. The difference between the blankness of old maps and the blankness of the new map is this: In the new, we have transcended hope, that human addiction which feeds and destroys us, cheers us on and cheats us. Explorers, lovers, and children hope, but always the trail runs out.

In the interior, it continues to snow heavily—two and one-half feet in Denali National Park, with another foot forecast. The park is now blocked to visitors, including those who had special September driving permits. The crystals of snow and ice in their infinity of shapes fall upon the parklands and the mountain—still officially called McKinley, not Denali; the mountain Walter Harper was first to climb. The crystals fall on the crevasses and those who rest within them.

In our living room, by the front door, I go up to a hanging framed photograph of McKinley, take it down, and examine it. My friend John took it the same year Tom climbed the mountain. I gave it to Tom for Christmas. In the photograph, inscrutable clouds cap the peak. I can really concentrate only on the colorful tundra in the foreground: a blue creek runs through brown grasses and bushes. In the middle ground, where tall trees grow, shadows pool. Beyond, the mountain explodes, an unimaginable tidal wave of light and shade, the eternal dance.

When Tom returned from his successful climb, he showed slides in the living room. We waited late, that summer night, until it was dark, then put up a sheet for a screen. I lay on the chintz-covered couch with a quilt, grateful that I could experience the mountain that way, well fed and warm. I have no desire to hike long distances or to camp out. I am almost constantly cold and have no tolerance for hypothermic conditions. I want, and need, home and the familiar: a soft, warm bed (ours is a heated waterbed), the comfort of someone beside me whose every sound and move I know and who serves as my furnace—someone who will take my shockingly cold hands and put them under his arms without complaint. There thinking ends, and the body finds its way.

Once, when we were much younger and Sam was a toddler in a pack on our backs, we climbed Mount Juneau, turning back just below the summit, when the ice got too difficult. I have never tried it again, though the mountain looms over my house and me. I am content to watch it, reading its shadows and colors, its moods and its weathers.

Downtown, two ships tie up at the dock on an afternoon grown both sunny and windy. It is the place where the bodies from the *Princess Sophia* were brought ashore in late October and early November 1918, in the time of influenza, when, it is said, the prostitutes turned nurse.

Today the remains of Vitus Bering are reburied, with military honors, near his original gravesite on Bering Island, in the Komandorskie chain. In honor of the two hundred fiftieth anniversary of his expedition, his grave was found, his body exhumed, his skeleton examined, and a bust reconstructed from his skull at the Institute of Forensic Medicine in Moscow. It was a very different face from what we had been led to believe. The portrait we had gazed at all these years turned out to be that of his great-uncle, a poet and historiographer, for whom he had been named. Vitus Bering was somebody else.

We circle back, learning again what we thought we had known, learning that our map had been incomplete, that vast areas had been only imagined, that our instruments had been insufficient, our chronometer off, our unit of measurement different, our language different, our calendar different (Julian or Gregorian, civil or astronomical time, nautical day or non-nautical day). Once more the coastline had changed. We hadn't been where we thought we were.

Press on. Winter is coming.

SEPTEMBER 15

Rain and dark this morning. No birds.

Federal and state officials are registering more concern now about the nuclear waste dump site near Point Hope. High incidences of cancer among the Inupiat people of northwest Alaska, which have been explained away before, are now being given new consideration; the study by federal health officials will be reopened. The governor has visited the site and promised action.

Two southeastern legislators have each donated $500 for information leading to the arrest of the vandals who torched the Auke totem pole.

SEPTEMBER 16

Torrential rains have given way to sunshine, and a small flock of sparrows. Bright new snow glimmers on the mountains.

In Fairbanks, where heavy snow on branches has knocked down power lines, emergency shelters have been set up to provide refuge until repairs can be made.

In Talkeetna, near Denali National Park, Mike "Ace" Ebling, a retired Air Force sergeant who won two Purple Hearts in Vietnam, finishes preparing a monument for the cemetery he tends. The white-painted telephone pole, with the figures of two climbers near the top, commemorates the seventy-five climbers killed during the last sixty years of challenging McKinley. More than ninety have died in this period on McKinley and neighboring peaks and glaciers. Ebling remembers, especially, Terrance "Mugs" Stump, who fell into a crevasse on May 21, the seventh of eleven mountain fatalities this season. It was Mugs who got him going on this chainsaw work, a tribute he had thought about for some years.

SEPTEMBER 17

Faint northern lights last night have been replaced by thick clouds moving down the mountainsides.

✳ *A body has been found in Harris Harbor, Juneau, where we walked along the docks last night explaining different gear types to a visitor.* There has been no claim for a missing person. *It is not the body of Walter B. Shaw, the seventy-two-year-old tourist who disappeared from the* Sagafjord *in July; it is apparently that of a man approximately twenty-five years old.* Identification found on the body indicates that it might be a Juneau man who has not been seen for about five weeks. The man was not reported missing because his friends and family thought he was traveling. An autopsy is being conducted.

On a beach at Shelikof Bay, near Sitka, hikers have found a body in a survival suit that might be one of the missing men from the Mary May, *lost during the halibut opening.*

In Anchorage, state troopers say they are close to identifying the body of the hiker who starved to death on the Stampede Trail. The man is said to have come from South Dakota.

Mount Spurr has erupted again, and I think of Gayle Roth. The cloud of volcanic ash this time has blown north of Anchorage into the Matanuska Valley. There will be no darkening of the Malaspina and Bering glaciers to the south, only the falling of snow.

And everywhere within the higher latitudes, winter closes in.

SEPTEMBER 18

Rain, less heavy, continues to fall, and Gold Creek rages with the torrents coming down off the mountain. I take my friend Edith to the ferry; she is heading for Skagway and then home to New Mexico. She will see little today; the mountains have disappeared in cloud. As I return, I see three fat robins bathing in two mud puddles.

More snow is expected in Fairbanks.

Juneau police continue to seek the identity of the body of the young man found floating in the boat basin two days ago. There are still no claims for missing persons.

SEPTEMBER 19

Rain falls heavily. In Fairbanks, snow continues.

The Stampede Trail hiker has been identified. His name is Christopher McCandless, known as Alex. He was a twenty-four-year-old graduate of Emory University, where he studied psychology and philosophy. From Annandale, Virginia, he had spent a short time with Wayne Westerberg, a wheat farmer in Madison, South Dakota, who had picked him up as a hitchhiker and given him a short-term job. He left journals with Westerberg that outlined travels around the country during 1990 and 1991. The journals noted that he had burned the last of his money in the Arizona desert and had been run out of town by the police in Astoria, Oregon.

On April 27, McCandless sent a postcard with a picture of a polar bear to his friend and benefactor in South Dakota: "This is the last you'll hear from me, Wayne. Please return all mail I receive to the sender. It might be a very long time before I return south. If this adventure proves fatal and you don't ever hear from me again, I want you to know you are a great man." The message ends, "I now walk into the wild." It was signed "Alex."

A family spokesperson in Annandale commented, "We appreciate the interest in Chris—how he lived and how he spent his last days. But because Chris was an intensely private person, his family and friends are respecting his privacy and have no further comment at this time."

The body recovered from Shelikof Bay has been identified as that of Robert D. Enloe, twenty-three, of Coeur d'Alene, Idaho, a crewman aboard the Mary May, *last seen in rough weather in Sitka Sound on September 9.*

＊ *The Coast Guard reports that the body of a man in a survival suit has been found on the south shore of Middleton Island, just south of Prince William Sound and eighty miles southwest of Cordova.* He has not been identified, but this could be a crew member of the *Sea Breeze*.

The mayor of Barrow, Don Long, has taken his first bowhead whale since becoming a whaling captain seven years ago—the tenth of the season taken by Barrow's whalers. The Alaska Whaling Commission reports that another crew struck and lost a whale the same day.

＊ *The Coast Guard has called off the search for a humpback whale that became tangled in a fishing net near Berner's Bay, thirty miles north of Juneau.* The whale got caught in the gill net of *Aries,* a fishing boat from Haines. By the time a Coast Guard cutter, rescue divers, and a federal marine mammal specialist got to the area, the whale had disappeared. "Either the whale got rid of the net or the whale drowned," a Coast Guard spokesperson said. "We don't know which." Later, six humpback whales were seen in the area.

Disappearances in the natural world are seldom recognized and rarely recorded. One exception was an incident during the summer of 1992 witnessed by two fishermen from Gustavus, not far from Berner's Bay, and related to reporters. They watched a pod of orcas, or killer whales, chase two moose swimming Icy Strait from Chichagof Island to the mainland. The orcas attacked and ate one moose while the second swam away into a kelp bed, where it found protection. For an hour the orcas tried to pursue the struggling moose, but they could not break through the kelp. By the time they gave up their pursuit, the exhausted moose had drowned, unable to free itself from the entangling plants. Later its body washed up on shore.

We leave the house in not quite two months.

In the morning I write, in the afternoon take care of daily tasks, and at night sort and throw out. It is easier then, in the dark, when I am tired and out of patience.

To those who have stolen from my heart and my life, I say this: Take it. Feed on what pieces you have. I have enough. I am strong. Now we can go our separate ways.

Who, what, is left?

I remember the funeral of my aunt. Her unkind husband was having her buried in his family mausoleum near Brownwood, Texas, far from New York, where she had lived all her life and belonged. A priest came from Waco. He said, "There is nothing but for us to be kind to each other and to love one another." As he spoke, I looked out over the sparse rangeland, where a few sheep grazed. It was enough. As he sprinkled holy water on the coffin, the drops caught sun and filled with light and color.

CHAPTER XIV

Winter Takes Hold

1992: SEPTEMBER 22 – OCTOBER 4

SEPTEMBER 22

Autumn comes with sun and broken clouds. A flock of birds is passing through. I am glad they have sunshine, no wind.

Today the *Westerdam* visits, one of the last of the ships carrying tourists. Tomorrow the *Sky Princess*, carrying twelve hundred passengers, is scheduled to be the last. When the ship pulls away at noon, the channel will be empty of large ships for the next eight months. The *Sky Princess* is a day late because of bad weather encountered off the British Columbia coast. Winter is closing in; it is time for visitors to have left the high latitudes.

In the 1870s, whalers at this time were running for the Bering Strait and escape to the ice-free seas.

SEPTEMBER 23

Cloudy skies, cold temperatures. Last night a friend told me it had been down to eight degrees in Soldotna, on the Kenai Peninsula. This morning I saw a thrush on its way to Central America, but there are no flocks today. Gardeners are digging up dahlia bulbs, burying their cutback roses. The channel, the sky, the gardens, go empty. The colors and sounds of summer disappear. The empty hummingbird feeders swing in the breeze. I wonder how far those smallest and most pugnacious of birds have gotten. I think of how Lady Franklin's niece, in her journal of their springtime visit to Sitka, remarked on how the Tlingits captured hummingbirds and sold them, their legs tied to sticks. Lady Franklin never found the papers she sought, nor news of her husband's expedition, but she did leave behind in Sitka a number of copies of McClintock's account of the voyage of the *Fox* that she had bankrolled.

According to Sophia Cracroft, a bemused young soldier who called himself Prince Thoreau held great admiration for Lady Franklin, bringing her flowers and seeking to have her read his journal. He claimed he had seen her husband's spirit over the mountains the night she arrived and offered to communicate with that spirit if she provided an object that would be familiar to the lost explorer. All we know is that she declined but treated him kindly, giving him a small knife.

Now in the northern tundra, people search in the ancient way for *masru*, a kind of root which mice collect and cache in their underground burrows. It is very important when you remove the pieces of root not to remove them all; otherwise the mice will die and will not be able to collect for you in the future. Your life might well depend on the kindness of mice. It is important to leave something in exchange, such as a piece of dried fish. Among the Yupik people, girls used to be given a bracelet of mice hands to make their own hands nimbler.

Once I had a pet mouse, which escaped a number of times and found me in bed; it came right to my head, as if it had something to tell me. It is buried now, behind the house—the north end, just on the other side of the wall that makes our headboard.

As I walk uptown I encounter a wounded thrush on the sidewalk, across the street from the back of the Governor's Mansion. The bird, unable to fly, hops through a white picket fence into a yard. I speak to it; it hops off, not wanting to be any closer. I tell it I will check it when I return. I continue uptown, visit the dock area. Two ships are in, the *Rotterdam* and the *Dawn Princess*. There is no sign of the *Sky Princess*. I do not know what happened to the delayed ship or whether it will show up.

On the way home, I check on the yard where I last saw

the bird. It is empty. I walk on. How many birds have fallen, I wonder, on their way south? How many salmon have swum out of the school, out of the locator beacon of their spawning stream? How many stars have darkened? How many lost moons and lost islands, never there but only imagined, have dropped out of the charts? How many solitary explorers seeking what is known only to them have fallen off the map? And how many maps full of errors have blown away like birds in a storm, their makers disgraced and forgotten, the maps of their bones scattered?

The lost bird stays in my mind. From the earliest times, birds have been more than symbols of hope to explorers. They have been markers on the map of the unknown. If a large flock of migrating birds had not darkened the skies for Columbus when they did, he might well have had to give in to his mutinous crew and turn back to Spain before reaching the Americas. With the birds—clearly not seabirds—he could rally his men, convince them that land was not far off, and keep going. The birds are thought to have been Eskimo curlews, now possibly extinct.

Almost from the time De Long set out on his doomed expedition, he looked for birds as an omen. First there was the tomtit sent out in a bottle; then, close to the end, in the starvation of the Lena River delta, he wrote: "When we halted at noon for dinner a little snow-bird flew around us and finally lighted upon my flagstaff which I carry. Mr. Collins immediately exclaimed, 'That is good luck, Captain.' Such small things even are noticeable in our kind of life." One of the last vignettes recorded is that of the seagull landing on the flagpole that the party put up in hopes of attracting attention. Though no one came, a seagull did, and provided yet another meal.

I become more conscious of birds. I know they bring news as well as portents. It is news I cannot understand but feel compelled to record. It is part of the map of disappearance. It has to do with concentrating on small things, celebrating beauty: the oracle of hollow bones.

A bird can be a compass, as can a pussywillow—if only we allow ourselves to observe, and have faith in ourselves as readers and interpreters, as creators of our world.

* * *

✳ *In Anchorage, a nineteen-year-old college student is reported missing after a week of odd behavior.* Josh Howard, whose eager face smiles out from the newspaper, was a happy, well-liked, and thoroughly engaged student. Recently he began to talk and act in an unusual manner, speaking of a special energy. Then, suddenly, he was gone. Family and friends have twice searched the woods near the parking lot where he parked his car.

I speak to my son Tom in Anchorage. A part-time student and business manager of the student newspaper at the University of Alaska, Anchorage, he is well aware of Josh's disappearance. He was sitting next to the paper's editor when the editor called Josh's stepfather for an interview.

Here in Juneau, the body in the harbor has been identified: twenty-five-year-old Gregory Reaves, of Juneau. He was not reported missing because he was thought to be out of town. The official cause of death is drowning. His body was found by a passerby.

From time to time overwintering rufous hummingbirds are reported in nearby woods. They are meant to be in Mexico. But I do not doubt the word of the hunters who say they have come across them.

There is a theory that all animals have an equal number of heartbeats in their lifetime. Those heartbeats come at different speeds. I think of the bowhead whale at Barrow and the rufous hummingbird beating its way along the stormy southeast Alaska coast, its heart going perhaps as fast as its wings.

I think of Lady Franklin and the hummingbird, another bird of good omen. It was early for hummingbirds when she got to Sitka; her mail had been misdirected to Kodiak, and she missed that too. When she left Sitka, she traveled south, just as the hummingbirds were traveling north. Her farthest point fell short by many latitudes of her husband's, but what that exact point was we cannot know, probably never will. What wordless geography is this—a blankness telling us that Earth is a symbol, our journeyings are but invisible marks?

This is the geography of Lady Sarashina: the bridge of dreams. Sarashina: a mountainous area the writer obliquely refers to but does not name. This becomes her name. Scholars have decided. She herself is lost, her name long gone. Only her dreams remain, anchored to earth by the weighty notes of commentators, unable to fly.

A bridge of dreams. Akbar, the wise Mogul emperor of sixteenth-century India, exhorted, "Life is a bridge; cross it but build no house on it."

SEPTEMBER 24

Partly clear skies have given way to solid cloud, rain and wind expected. A few sparrows fly through the neighborhood. I come across a flock of varied thrushes where I found the single one yesterday. The *Sky Princess* makes its last call in Juneau, and the channel goes empty. Nearly three hundred thousand tourists have come and gone this past season. Most have returned home by now.

One summer day in the Alaska Airlines freight warehouse, as I was attending to the shipping of a bicycle, I found myself standing next to a coffin; suitcases were strapped to the top.

SEPTEMBER 25

The body found on Middleton Island, eighty miles southwest of Cordova, has been identified as that of Walter J. Prichard, thirty-five, of Yakutat, owner-operator of the Sea Breeze.

Two crew members are still missing: David Harris, forty-three, of Seward, and Jay David Mattila, twenty-three, of Minnesota.

SEPTEMBER 26

Clouds, blue patches, showers. A few sparrows: I see white on their tails.

The whalers of Barrow have landed their eleventh bowhead of the season, but whalers in Wainwright, eighty-five miles to the southwest, are still waiting for the migration. Wainwright captains say the whales seem to be migrating unusually far to the north as they head west.

Farther down the coast, the whalers of Point Hope look for a right-leaning new moon, the whaling moon.

SEPTEMBER 27

Rain, with an edge to the weather, a sense of the earth turning toward winter.

＊ *The Coast Guard has called off the search for twenty-six-year-old Anthony Evans, one of three on board an eighteen-foot Boston whaler that capsized in Kasaan Bay, near Ketchikan, to the south.* A second passenger was found dead on the hull, the third alive on the shore of an island in the bay.

In the papers, ads offering a cash reward for information about Josh Howard, still missing in the middle of Anchorage, have started to appear. No leads have been found.

A fire last month at Burnt Mountain, on the edge of the

Arctic National Wildlife Refuge, made known the existence of ten nuclear-powered electrical generators operated by the Air Force. Again state and Native leaders are expressing amazement and anger, demanding that the potential threat be removed.

Kemp Houck, director of the watchdog group Atoms and Waste, happened upon the revelation while reading at the Nuclear Regulatory Commission. It came in the form of a computer message from the Air Force warning the commission that the unguarded generators were in the path of the fire and could be dangerous.

Air Force officials claim that the generators—radioisotope thermoelectric generators—are safe. The first one went into operation on the mountain in 1973. Senator Frank Murkowski of Alaska holds a seat on the Intelligence Committee but claims he was unaware of the devices.

The area, used for subsistence hunting by the Gwichin people, is near the wintering grounds of the Porcupine caribou herd, which numbers more than two hundred thousand. This herd is at the heart of the controversy over possible drilling in the Arctic National Wildlife Refuge. The rhythm of the north goes on.

SEPTEMBER 28
Leaden skies, with the prediction of rain and high winds by night. I notice very few birds. I look out at the new snow on the mountain peaks. No matter what we might do

or think, winter presses down on us. The birds that have not escaped by now are in danger, as once the steam whalers that waited too long on the northernmost coast were in danger. Land Otter Men roam the stormy shoreline, and Southeast Woman, who brings bad weather, rules: The prevailing winter winds are east-southeast.

I bring inside our red, white, and black yin-yang windsock, which flies before the bright red front door. The hanging baskets of fuchsia I leave to the elements; sometimes they continue to bloom until snow falls here at the foot of Mount Juneau.

SEPTEMBER 29

Heavy rain, accompanied by increasing winds. Leaves rip from the trees and fill the sky like flocks. I see one varied thrush in an alley.

The marbled murrelet is being added to the federal list of endangered species, by order of a federal court. The U.S. Fish and Wildlife Service is reluctant, claiming that further logging restrictions in old-growth forests will ensue. The marbled murrelet suffered severely from the *Exxon Valdez* oil spill. Only recently was it discovered to nest in old-growth forest. It is the old-growth forest that the timber industry seeks so ardently. It is the old-growth forest that the marbled murrelets need—as do the salmon, the Sitka black-tailed deer, the bears (both black and brown), the eagles, the martens, and many others.

The storm has passed. No birds appear.

Two of Alaska's three-member congressional delegation have demanded that the military remove the nuclear-powered generators from Burnt Mountain. They are requesting further that immediate testing be done to determine health and safety threats and that representatives from nearby villages be included in the inspection.

Ads for information about Josh Howard now run regularly in the papers. The reward money has increased to $5,500. A letter from a friend appears today, thanking the people of Alaska for their efforts in attempting to find Josh. He cites a number of specific examples, from personal encouragement to financial support from businesses, and closes: "I have been Josh's friend since fifth grade. I promise that neither Josh's family, friends, nor I will give up until Josh is returned to us safe and sound. [Signed] Greg Beaulieu."

OCTOBER 1

Dark though fairly calm skies. I come across a tiny sparrow—it must be the young of this year—in a mountain ash tree by a sidewalk near the Governor's Mansion. It is all alone and seems ready to listen to me talk. I wonder where its mother has gone, how long they have been separated, how far it has already traveled, how far it has yet to go, whether it will survive, and if not, who will notice.

I remember De Long, scanning the sky for birds, noting the ducks and geese and, with evident excitement, the exquisite Ross's gulls. And where did his bottled tomtit go, the message to the *Herald*, which was waiting instead for a big scoop?

On television I see a program on Wrangel Island, now a Russian preserve. There are the Ross's gulls in their other-worldly beauty, those rare birds of the drift ice. There are the polar bears. There are the foxes.

I watch from my warm waterbed. I think of the desperation of the *Karluk* party trying to survive there before Captain Bartlett returned, and the suicide of Breddy, who had given up all hope. I pull more covers around me.

On our bed, on top of blankets, rests the yin-yang dragon quilt made by our artist friend Judy Cooper. It clearly depicts Martin and me curled in the tail of the immense dragon in the center. We are the eye of the dragon's curled tail. Judy made it for us to commemorate the book she illustrated for me, *On Why the Quilt-Maker Became a Dragon*. Between this quilt and warm water I float to sleep and wake to the sounds of rain, wind, or silence.

Today the paper reports that nineteen Aleutian Canada geese are being transported on the weekly Aeroflot flight from Anchorage to Magadan in a program that will reintroduce the species to the Russian Far East, where they have become virtually extinct. Magadan is the port on the Sea of Okhotsk through which the Kolyma prisoners filed for distribution to the camps. Perhaps someday the real map of

Kolyma will be drawn; primary sources will be found, and we will circle back to learn what we thought we had always known or would not allow ourselves to know. As Varlam Shalamov, a survivor and chronicler of the gold camps, tells us, the countless bodies lie there still in their mass graves, well protected by the permafrost, a permanent portrait, and on the left shin of each is a plywood tag with the prisoner's case number written forever in graphite. It is all there, a record waiting for us, if we dare to go and read it: a cairn of enormous tragedy—with another cairn ten feet true north and yet another and another.

Some of the ships that carried the prisoners there were formerly named the *Puget Sound*, the *Dallas*, the *Bellingham*. And the *Exxon Valdez*, lest anyone be unaware, is now the *Sea River Mediterranean*.

In our living room, in a case of crystal and antique china, I keep vials of oil I collected from a beach in Prince William Sound in April 1989, when I went to the oil spill as part of my job for the Department of Fish and Game. Every so often I pick these vials up. I hear the cries of the dying sea otters being transported in trucks from water to rescue station. At night, in the sharp cold, those cries pierced my being. I got used to the mounds of dead animals, but never the cries of the otters. There are some things that need not to be forgotten.

* * *

It is raining hard. When walking the dog, I come across a dead bird—I think a young varied thrush—in the gutter under a car. Later, when I am shopping at Fred Meyer's, I hear a young girl next to me excitedly call to her mother, "Look, there's a bird!" I look but see nothing out of the ordinary. I keep looking, then see it: a sparrow in the celery. The sparrow appears very happy, pecking in the long light-green rows. I feel a rush of pleasure for it but know that pleasure cannot last. In a moment, startled by the attention it has received, it is up and flying, throughout the store.

I finish my shopping and leave, hurrying. Tonight Samantha Khury, an animal communicator from Los Angeles, is in town to give a lecture on how to deal with the black bears that wander into town and become habituated to garbage. Last summer, fourteen were shot in Juneau. Many summers ago, one took refuge in our black willow tree. Perhaps Samantha has a way of helping them know that they must not venture near us and our leavings.

At Samantha's lecture, I relearn the news: We can communicate with other species by recognizing that we are all soul. We can solve problems by visualizing, feeling, and knowing them to be solved.

OCTOBER 3

Samantha's workshop continues, with practical application: How do you, in real terms, send pictures back and forth to an animal? We begin by practicing person to person.

In Barrow, there is an increasing problem with polar bears, which are attracted to the town by the killing and butchering of what are now fourteen bowheads, the final harvest of the season. The pack ice has come in unusually early this year, bringing the bears with it. City officials plan to dispose of forty-five cubic yards of fat and other remains at sea and to bury three dumptruck loads at the end of the city road.

In 1923, when Ada Blackjack was left alone on Wrangel Island as the sole survivor of Stefansson's ill-planned colony, she lived in deep-seated fear of polar bears. Although she was small and had no construction experience, she built a platform over her tent so she could escape from the bears if need be. For her, bear was always listening; she would not say its name.

OCTOBER 4

At the worship service I attend, someone brings in a sparrow she found lying on the sidewalk. The sparrow is exhausted and appears unable to move. During the hour-long service, my friend, Ingrid, holds the bird and gently massages it with circles in the Tellington touch method, the method that releases past trauma from the cells. By the end of the program, the bird is perky and ready to go. We take it outside and carefully place it in a bush near a parking lot. It takes several minutes before it leaves Ingrid's hand.

I return to Samantha's workshop. She helps us first to acknowledge the soul of bear, the magnificence of bear, and to confront our fears.

Samantha has moved us out-of-doors, to a place where black bears have become a problem. We walk down an aquatic education trail in a stand of old-growth woods behind a school.

Samantha teaches us how to look for something that is lost. We stand, one by one, with eyes closed and move slowly in a circle, our hands extended. The left hand receives, the right hand projects. She tells us to concentrate on knowledge of ourselves as soul, projecting a beam of light from ourselves toward the woods, to locate the soul of bear. The purpose is not to draw in a bear but to communicate, soul to soul, with bear. I feel an intense area of light in one direction. Two others in the group do also. A bear does not appear—and that was not the intention—but Nancy and I particularly feel strongly the presence of bear. Later, after everyone has left, we go back to the dark and dripping woods and stand again in the clearing by the creek. There is the sound of water and the sound of birds; from far off, sounds of children, cars, and then an airplane. The presence has moved to a different location. We go to another part of the trail and stand on a platform at its end, looking out across a wet field where grass and flowers have lain down. The rain beats harder. In growing darkness we return through an avenue of invisible entities. The blueberry bushes glow with their yellow leaves and the old-growth forest holds its breath as we pass through.

As we come to the car, we are transfixed: Immediately before us a flock of robins, with at least one varied thrush, lands on a small berried tree. They quietly eat and look about. The rain beats down harder. Cars come and go. Children on bicycles pass by, talking. The birds stay.

Neither Nancy nor I could make a move. In spite of the cold pouring rain it would, as Nancy remarked later, have been rude to get into the car. We waited and watched as the birds ate, looked about, and, one by one, flew off.

The birds had come to us, and we had a powerful emotional contact. I thought of De Long—the snowbird on his flagstaff, the rare and beautiful Ross's gulls that found the *Jeannette* and provided contact with the world of flight and freedom. The birds told me: It is a continuum. We are all traveling together, creating our map; we cannot be lost.

When I got home I heard the news: The seventeen-year-old son of friends had attempted suicide. He had died that afternoon. His mother was away, in Anchorage. Martin was at the hospital when the boy's father made the decision to cut the life-support system.

I walked the dog in near darkness. The rain continued

to pelt down. Except for the rain, the world was silent. I remembered what Patricia had said when we walked on the Perseverance Trail: There are no spiritual disasters. I remembered Rasmussen, quoting the wisdom of the Caribou Eskimos: "No life once given can ever be lost or destroyed." I thought of the Natives of British Columbia whom Hugh Brody came to know—how they created maps with trails to heaven. I remembered Breddy, of the *Karluk* party on Wrangel Island, who shot himself with a handgun, as Chad did. It was June 25. Rescue came on September 7. But there was no rescue for Breddy and there was no rescue for Chad. We are left with the stab of mystery in our hearts and anguish for those left behind—the deserted. It is so hard to see!

Chad left a note. Part of it has been revealed, read at his funeral. He wanted us to believe in God. The Episcopal minister used the opportunity to disparage "Oriental" religions, saying they held no reverence for individual life. She was wrong, but it did not matter. Already Chad knew what she does not.

I tell myself over and over, no life once given can ever be lost or destroyed. One of the last great shamans told us.

Chad, like the young man who starved to death on the Stampede Trail, took his walk into the wild. We would not see either of them, but they had not disappeared.

RECORD 14

I took a practice trip—to Wells College, in Aurora, New York, for several days of readings and classes. It was the five hundredth anniversary of the voyages of Columbus to the New World, and the student body was engaged in lively expressions of antiexploitation. I tried to point out that Columbus had been a great navigator, a great seaman, a man who trusted to faith and to the flight of birds, a man who could have turned back if he had believed less. I would be sailing that winter in his islands.

Afterward, I visited Helen and India in New Paltz—the home of our Huguenot ancestors—and my mother in New York.

In six weeks, our friends the Gaffneys were going to move into our house. I wanted the animals to understand that we were not deserting them. It was especially important for Kaleb, the chocolate Lab. He had been abandoned by his first owner and would carry the scars for life. "I promise you, Kaleb," I said over and over. "We will never abandon you."

My friend John Jensen, a therapist, had said, When you know you need to say goodbye to someone, practice. I practiced and practiced. The animals smiled sweetly as I spoke to them. I could not tell whether what I said might save them from anxiety and sorrow as the door shut behind us and we drove off in the dark.

CHAPTER XV

Flying West of the Truth

O C T O B E R   8

Today it is reported that the Bering Glacier is reaching a "catastrophic retreat" phase, ejecting giant icebergs into the Gulf of Alaska in the path of the oil tankers moving down from Valdez. The head of the U.S. Geological Survey's international polar programs is quoted as saying, "The big concern is that the glacier is less than sixty miles away from Prince William Sound." Scientists expect large icebergs to continue breaking off for the next fifty to one hundred years.

OCTOBER 14

❋ *Two small planes with a total of five people aboard have been missing since they took off from Fairbanks three days ago.* A Piper PA-28 Cherokee took off Sunday at 6:30 P.M. for Anchorage, and an AR-58 Champ left at 1 P.M., filing no flight plan but said to be headed for Homer. One search, with twelve planes from the Alaska state troopers and the Civil Air Patrol, continues.

OCTOBER 15

❋ *Alaska state troopers have suspended a search for a nineteen-year-old Nome man who disappeared while moose hunting two weeks ago.* He was last seen in a cabin in Council, seventy-five miles northwest of Nome, on September 28.

The search for the two missing planes that took off from Fairbanks has widened. An Anchorage restaurant that two of the missing persons worked for has set up a fund to pay for rescue efforts and is giving other employees time off to assist in the search.

OCTOBER 16

Barrow has now harvested eighteen whales, and the problem with polar bears has grown worse. It appears that taking excess meat to the dump was a mistake. Two polar bears have had to be shot there. The authorities are now hazing the bears with snowmachines and a helicopter. Relocating the bears is being considered, but only as a desperate measure. Little is known about the movement of polar bears.

Every year, three to six hundred polar bears den on Wrangel Island, a major nursery for them. Cooperative research with the Russians started in 1989, when two Russian scientists visited the Alaska Fish and Wildlife Research Center. In 1990, three American biologists spent six weeks on Wrangel Island with their Russian colleagues, capturing and radio-collaring polar bears.

It was these bears the two U.S. Fish and Wildlife Service biologists, Bevins and Menkens, were tracking when they disappeared on the pack ice in October 1990. Since then, new generations have come out of the dens and hunted over thousands of miles of ice.

The fall whaling season has been a very good one for Barrow, one to make up, in part, for the poor spring season. In the spring only two whales were taken, and the second one with tragedy. On May 28, as that whale was being pulled onto the ice, a pulley broke loose and shot into the crowd, killing two women and injuring a third.

Later, biologists found that the whale had pieces of a stone blade embedded in her back—part of a harpoon point of a type not used for a hundred years. They said, moreover, that the whale must have been at least twenty years old when the blade entered her flesh a century ago; otherwise she would have been too small to hunt. It is not known how old bowheads live to be, but Barrow elders called the whale "tippulaayuk," meaning "You can't even put it on a calendar." The take struck deep into the hearts of the village. The butchering of the ancient whale was done quietly, without anyone's calling out the usual praise to the captain, and some of those to whom the meat was given would not eat it.

I think of my whaling forebears from Nantucket. Maybe one of them had chased this animal and witnessed her escape, her disappearance into the icy waters of a place he was ready to leave forever.

And I think of the English whaler and explorer William Scoresby, who brought back from the Arctic drawings of ninety-six snow crystals that he had observed in the high latitudes of Greenland. His book, *An Account of the Arctic Regions with a History and Description of the Northern Whale Fisheries,* was published in Edinburgh in 1820. It fanned the passion for completing the Northwest Passage, the passion that led Franklin into the blankest of maps.

It is the twentieth anniversary of the disappearance of Boggs and Begich in their plane en route from Anchorage to Juneau. Pegge Begich, widow of Nick Begich, reminisces. "I wish there were answers," she says. "My children wish there were answers." Twice she ran for her husband's congressional seat and lost. Now she plans to leave Alaska and return to Minnesota, where she met Begich. Their son Tom plans to travel to Icy Bay next summer to search in the area where the recently unearthed FBI reports state that

262

sophisticated tracking equipment found the wreckage with two survivors.

Icy Bay, near Yakutat, is not far from Lituya Bay, the land ruled by the Spirit of Lituya. It lies between the Malaspina Glacier and the Bering Glacier and points toward Mount St. Elias. It is surrounded on three sides by towering and moving ice.

OCTOBER 20

During my practice run in New York, I visit the Cooper-Hewitt's new exhibit, "The Power of Maps." It tells me

One place can be mapped many ways.
Maps are useful, but never neutral.
Maps are social reconstructions of reality.
Take the power of maps into your own hands.

I see what happens when you put Australia on the top instead of on the bottom of the map; what happens when you map incidents of disease or accident; what happens when you locate heaven and hell; what happens when you dream.

Once Captain Bartlett lost a chart at a critical moment. He was piloting the *Roosevelt* for Peary, homeward bound after an early attempt on the pole, in 1905. Off Labrador, in a storm, the wind seized the chart out of Bartlett's hands. It was the only chart of the area he had. He stopped the ship and had a boat lowered. The crew chased after the paper for some minutes. But just before they reached it, it sank. There was nothing to do but go on without a chart. Somehow they got safely to port. That port was named Hopedale.

OCTOBER 22

On this day in 1985, a Learjet crashed in the Chilkats as it approached the Juneau airport. It hit the mountains close to where Alaska Airlines Flight 1866 went down in 1971, near Teardrop Lake—so close that a federal investigator called for a beacon to be installed there on the mountaintop. The plane was on its way from Anchorage to Juneau to pick up a pregnant woman and take her to an Anchorage hospital for specialized treatment. Four died. Again, the crew apparently thought they were closer to the airport than they were, having radioed that they were near Gustavus. Like those on Flight 1866, they were approximately nine miles west of what they took to be the truth: a miscalculation that led to shattering impact and avalanche.

OCTOBER 23

On this day in 1918, the *Princess Sophia* departed from Skagway as the last ship out of the north that season; she was carrying miners from the Yukon and Christmas mail for the soldiers at the front in France. On November 11, when 156 southbound bodies from the *Sophia* were carried by her sister ship, *Princess Alice,* into Vancouver, it was Armistice Day. The Great War had ended. Walter Harper and his wife, Frances Wells, were left behind in Juneau, to lie in the shadow of Mount Juneau, near the grave of the town's founder, Joe Juneau.

It is possible to go into the state museum in Juneau, down into the basement archives, to see and hold the personal property collected from the wreck: rusted eyeglasses and keys, personal papers, and tickets—for the ride to freezing death. It is not a place most people see, or know about.

OCTOBER 24

The search for the two missing planes that took off from Fairbanks is over. During twelve days, state, federal, and civilian pilots have covered 56,600 square miles between Fairbanks and Homer. During one day, more than forty planes participated. No trace of either plane was found. On board the Cherokee were the pilot, Matthew Brewer, twenty-three; his girlfriend, Jennifer Kughn, twenty-three; and his parents, James and Betty Brewer, all of Anchorage. On board the smaller plane was the pilot, Timothy Young, thirty-two.

OCTOBER 26

As I return from my practice trip "outside," as we refer to anyplace beyond Alaska, I hear on the car radio that the body of Josh Howard has been found in woods near Anchorage. He was found by hikers walking on a trail in Campbell Creek Canyon, east of the city. Apparently he died of hypothermia. Reports indicate that he may have been on LSD, but toxicology reports have not been completed. It is reported that on the day before he disappeared, he claimed he wanted to "become one with the trees." The paper runs his obituary, with the suggestion that donations be sent to the Missing Children's Fund.

OCTOBER 27

✳ *A forty-seven-year-old woman is missing in Ketchikan.* A plane, helicopter, and search dog have been used in the attempt to find the woman, who may have gone hiking near her home. She has been missing for three days.

✳ *In Yakutat, the body of a man found on a beach has been identified as Lowell Preston, thirty-seven, a professional diver and commercial fisherman.* It is thought Preston died in a boating accident during a storm that produced fifty-knot winds a week ago.

Daylight Savings Time is gone, replaced by early darkness. Rain falls. In Anchorage, snow. The tracks of all who have walked the summer grow fainter, disappear. High above the mountains, crystals form and fall to earth. Over and over the magic of physics occurs—no two crystals exactly alike, but each doing the same job. And they do the job well, covering us, hiding us. They are the agents of disappearance, the handwork of cold and of time. To them we are equal, whether we are known or unknown, whether the planes go out for us once or a thousand times, whether we are front-page copy or filler. The crystals know the ultimate secret: All in the universe is equal. The tracks of bears on their high trails disappear with the tracks of planes and their people. All go under the universal blanket of white.

OCTOBER 28

The body of Diane Wyatt of Ketchikan has been found wrapped in a tarp and under water near a sawmill. Her husband has been arrested for her murder. Statistics now make up her epitaph, keep her name alive as a woman who suffered the ultimate domestic abuse.

OCTOBER 29

Anchorage has had a heavy snowfall, and power continues to be out in some areas.

Maria Iverson calls me. She has just spoken to Gayle Roth, a friend of some years. She suggests that I call Gayle. I think about this. Should I intrude? I need to enter the empty space.

It is the day when the whaler *Helen Mar* escaped through Bering Strait in 1879, carrying the crew of the lost *Mercury* and after losing sight forever of the *Mount Wallaston* and the *Vigilant,* with which she had also traveled in convoy. She too had been given up for lost. It was one of the latest dates of southbound passage made by a whaling ship in that century. She might well have been one of the ships to pursue the ancient bowhead killed in Barrow last spring, the whale that could have been 120 years old, or more.

I call Gayle. Gayle tells me how sure she is that her husband, Jeff, and the other four men, including my friend Kent, are alive and are all coming back alive. Another of the wives, Jane Barber, is also sure. She stays open, she says, to dreams—hers and those of others. Right now she has two planes searching an area that she has triangulated from dreams. Those who have visions call. Four have coincided. In the first hours of knowing of the disappearance, Gayle says, she and a friend independently had the same vision, of all five men walking on a certain kind of terrain —hay-colored—a terrain of the physical plane, she assured me. She felt nothing to disturb her, as she did when her parents died, not long before the disappearance. On the contrary, she felt herself in a bubble of assurance. Gayle says she was not a churchgoing person but now she meditates and benefits from those meditations. The five men all loved one another deeply, she asserts. "I know my husband did not panic. I know he was able to land that plane," she states. "And if he landed the plane, they can survive."

My heart is torn for Gayle. I want to believe her, but this mystery belongs to the universe. I think of the glaciers, the crevasses, the heavily falling snow, the thorough and democratic snow which covers all with equal effectiveness. I remember something, words struggling to be called forth, and find *Dubliners*. I read the last sentence of "The Dead," as Gabriel awakens: "His soul swooned slowly as he heard the snow falling faintly through the universe and faintly falling, like the descent of their last end, upon all the living and the dead."

Soon the snow will move down from the mountains and fall on us here by the sea. It will fall equally on all of us, on the living and the dead—on the Harpers and on Chad and on those of us who are left trying to understand, trying to read, and make, the map, with all of its overlays and legends, its symbols and interpretations.

This was the day when De Long, dying of starvation on the Lena River delta in 1881, wrote his last journal entry. It was the day when the *Jeannette*'s doctor reported in 1879 his curious dream of being in the company of the Franklin expedition. Franklin told him that the only new invention that seemed of worth was the telephone. But how can the telephone help us now? It has enabled me to call Gayle Roth in Anchorage; beyond that, I do not know.

OCTOBER 31

John Active, the Yupik writer, comments in a column in the *Anchorage Daily News* that the Yupik word for October translates as "the month of the spirits of the dead." It is the month when inhabitants of southwest Alaska have long celebrated Qaariitaarvik, or the bladder ceremony, when the bladders of all the animals caught during the year are brought inside the men's house to be honored. As he says, "You see, we Yupik believe that every living thing on earth and in the heavens has a spirit, and we believe the spirits, or *yua*, of the animals dwell in these bladders, so even the bladders of sparrows, which little boys had caught with their bows and arrows, were hung with the others."

The Yupiks believed that an animal would give itself to a hunter when it deemed conditions to be right. The delicate balance of life depended on honoring the animals that so gave themselves. Whale or sparrow, equal honor was due. During this feast at the end of October, each bladder, containing the spirit, was returned to the sea, so that more animals might give themselves to the hunters the following year.

NOVEMBER 1

For the Tlingits, November is the Digging Month, the month when bears dig into their winter dens to hibernate.

Kah Lituya calls his slaves home.

Here in our living room, Alexander begins his hibernation, curling into a tighter and tighter ball. I would join him in my own way, in my heated waterbed under the quilt. I would be curled with my mate in the curl of the dragon's tail, forever and forever and forever—the River Merchant's Wife. Looking back, after long separation, she recalls:

> *At fifteen I stopped scowling.*
> *I desired my dust to be mingled with yours*
> *Forever and forever and forever.*
> *Why should I climb the lookout?*

Instead, I do what I can to push back the suffocating darkness. I get up early, hours before the light of dawn starts its tenuous way up Gastineau Channel, between the mountains. (In a month, if it is visible, the sun will barely scale the peaks before falling back into the Pacific.) I take a very hot shower—we have two shower heads in our one tub and a large supply of dangerously hot water. Revived, I do my meditations, with Alexander, whose life is nothing but prayer. Then I make tea—a pot of tea, a good black tea, Lapsang souchong the ultimate pleasure. I set it out on the cloth on the dining room table with cup and saucer, spoon, pitcher of milk, honey. I prefer a silver spoon. As much as possible, everything must match, especially since the table under the cloth is wobbly and scarred. We bought it from our neighbor Bob Garrison for five dollars soon after we moved into this house in the shadow of the black willow, the house the *Malaspina* brought me to.

After everything is set out, I light candles, red candles. And on the kitchen window ledge over the sink I light small red candles—part of *feng shui*—to help achieve balance with earth, to be in harmony with the house spirits. Every step is important. It pushes back the dark, which has risen now to flood stage, which could bear everything away in an instant.

NOVEMBER 4

✳ *After nine hours, a search was suspended for a crewman who fell off a crab vessel in the Bering Sea about a hundred miles north of Unimak Island.* Mike Ilti, twenty-seven, of Denver, fell overboard around midnight after his foot got caught in a line connected to a crab pot. According to the Coast Guard, the water temperature in the area is about forty-one degrees, and survival time is about fifteen minutes.

NOVEMBER 5

The medical reports on Josh Howard are complete. He was not under the influence of alcohol or drugs when he died. He died of hypothermia, frozen to death by the trail.

✳ *The search has widened for an airman missing for five days from the King Salmon Air Force Base, on the Alaska Peninsula not far from Lake Iliamna.* Bristol Bay Borough police chief Floyd Steele has commented, "We have absolutely no leads." The search will now be extended beyond the five-square-mile area around the base toward Naknek.

NOVEMBER 6

I visit Maria. We discuss Gayle Roth. Maria knows that Jeff Roth, his brothers, and their friends are dead. When she is thinking of Jeff, an indescribable sense of coldness grips the upper part of her body. In the lower part she feels nothing. Is this because his body was severed? she asks. She sees a place both very deep and dark: a crevasse? She senses that their bodies are on the Malaspina Glacier. Gayle is looking in the wrong place, over in Canada. As long as we discuss the Roths, the coldness grips Maria. She shows me her hands: They are shaking.

NOVEMBER 8

Under misty skies, I walk Kaleb. I begin to hear a familiar sound, a trilling. No, I think, it is too early, three weeks before Thanksgiving. But the trilling, like a chorus of bells, grows louder. I look up. There, in an alleyway of berried mountain ash trees—a flock of bohemian waxwings. I look for their delicate crests against the sky. There is no mistake. They have come early this year. I do not know what this means. I file it away for the map. It is the map inside my heart, the one that leads to heaven. It is hard to draw this map. It is hard even to speak of it. I struggle to open it up. See all the trails, and where they lead. See the places of good hunting, the places of accident, of success, of loss, the chasms of sorrow that cannot be filled, the bridge of dreams that falls short.

My friend Cy Peck, Jr., a Tlingit brought up as a Presbyterian, might be called a shaman or a medicine man— "one who knows the way." He calls himself neither but serves as a catalyst for healing by giving ceremonies in the Native American tradition. Each of us is on a journey, Cy says. Each of us is responsible for choosing how we make that journey; and these choices are within us. The ceremony, he says, helps us to make those choices by clarifying where we stand on earth. The orientation is to the directions of the heart, not of the compass. During the ceremony, he says, Old Crooked Beak is beside us. The drum speaks as a temple bell speaks.

I try to listen as we move deeper into winter and closer to the time of our departure. The ceremony I attend now is one of excision—cutting away the excess. Already I have left job, titles, salary, office routine, colleagues, the sure knowledge of how my day will be every day. Now I must throw down clothes, artifacts, paper. I make more piles— what to discard, what to give away, what to save. I collect and fill boxes, which I pack tightly into the attic, the attic over the west garden, where the lilies have gone to sleep.

I am there one night when I hear a rustle. I become

aware of Lady Sarashina retreating into the shadows. It is time for her to travel on: another pilgrimage. I am on my own.

NOVEMBER 9

Snow is now heavy in Anchorage. ✳ *Two men, near the city, have been killed in an avalanche.* One was training for a trip to the Himalayas.

Scientists have issued a red alert for Mount Spurr. It appears ready to explode again, at any time.

NOVEMBER 10

Snow is falling now in Juneau, though not yet sticking on the ground.

In contemplation, I ask for a sign. When I open my eyes, I see a robin on the crabapple tree outside the window. It is alone. It waits quietly for a long time, perhaps resting, perhaps listening for a signal. I wonder how it has come to be there, alone, in the desolation of winter; but I know it came for me.

I visit the Coast Guard to ask some questions about magnetic variation. They suggest that I look at some aeronautical charts for the gulf coast area. I go out to the Flight Service Center that the Federal Aviation Administration operates at the airport. It is snowing heavily as I open the door to the new building. Inside, I find myself in a large dark room filled with banks of monitors and instruments.

Video pictures of the world, with storms swirling over it, move in the semidarkness. Half the world, tilted, is visible, with clouds streaming over it, mostly on the top. Numbers flow rapidly on screens. Employees answer phones, give weather reports, tell pilots about other pilots. One pilot, I overhear, is on the ground in Skagway, waiting for heavy snow to clear.

I spread out the maps that will show me the gulf coast —the trip between Juneau and Anchorage by way of Yakutat. There is a great deal of empty space. I read the small lavender warnings for magnetic variations—up to 50 degrees near Annette Island, down by Ketchikan; at one point on the south end of Douglas Island, near me, 170 degrees. Mostly it is about six to ten degrees. But I have already been told by the Coast Guard that it goes as high as thirty degrees. And it changes *daily*. The "dark and great powers" are at work.

I look at the huge white area of the glaciers—the Malaspina and the Bering—and behind the Bering, the Bagley icefield. It is blank. I see nothing. I had been hoping for a vision, a sense of knowingness. I wanted to be able to point—there! It is there! You will find the plane there! Gayle, you can rest; Maria, you can rest. Everyone can stop dreaming, searching, hoping. But it does not happen. The maps lie flat on the counter, silent.

Several employees run from their screens to the front door and step out to look at the raging snowsquall. The satellite views of the world's storms continue without them, unmonitored. Soon, having folded the maps in front of me, I too go out into the squall, a thick white wind.

I drive by the airport. A small plane with floats is coasting down to the end of the runway. The snow is lessening, but the sky to the south is almost black. It is two o'clock in the afternoon, still weeks before the winter solstice, but darkness is everywhere. I hope the pilot knows when to take off, when and where to set down.

NOVEMBER 11

In a week we leave this house for the winter, leaving our beloved dog and cat with friends who will take our place. I am busy throwing out what I can, packing away what I cannot. I throw out many letters, some wrenching to hold. I do not touch my father's but look at them out of the corner of my eye. That is where, mystics say, it happens— that slight movement beyond the physical. But I simply cannot look at the letters directly and push them back against a cold stone wall. A bitter divorce, a family cut off: It should not have meant silence, such a break in the trail.

Once, when we heard he was dying, we flew back to New York to see him. His possessive new wife hovered; we could not really talk, but I took furtive looks at the furniture, the artwork—the Audubons and Currier and Iveses I had grown up with. How strange their setting now. I tried to tell him something about the work I was doing; I thought he would be pleased. He had wanted to be a poet but instead had gone to Wall Street after the Depression to support his family. He had commuted for many years, something he exhorted us not to do.

At the end of that strange, strained visit, we let the children feed ducks at the water's edge; then we left. My brother went to see him in the hospital just before he died. By then, though he indicated he wanted to, he could not talk. I do not know where he is buried.

Once, in our basement, we had a metal drum for burning attached to the furnace. What we burned in it helped keep the basement warm enough for me to go on writing there. Once, during an infestation, my family threw the dead bodies of mice in. Once, on top of those bones, I threw the letters of someone who had hurt me, dazed at the daring of such molten alchemy. One summer, while Martin and I were off on a trip, Tom called to say there had been a fire there. He was burning junk when the old head- and footboards stored near the furnace caught fire. It was Martin's father's mahogany bed, brought from Oyster Bay, originally from the house named Monomoit, where Martin lived as a child. We had never been able to fit it through the doors upstairs to get it into our small bedroom. Tom put out the fire with no further damage. The charred bed still awaits final disposition.

We are going to live for some months in Antigua, on board our sailboat, *Monomoit*. The name is a Cape Cod

Indian word meaning "place of crossings." It also stands for the chief of the local Indian tribe, who made a successful pact with William Nickerson when he arrived in the New World: In exchange for helping the immigrant and his family through their first winters, he was helped by them in his old age. Antigua is a post Sir John Franklin turned down before taking that of Tasmania and then returning to the Arctic.

This trip is part of retirement, part of what we have worked toward for a long time—the chance to live somewhere else during the long, dark winter. But now I wonder.

It is hard. I do not want to go on another trip, not yet. I do not even know whether I am back from the one I have been on. I am very tired. Sometimes, as I lift a box, a cup, a painting, as I push something deeper into the attic under the eaves, I see a face, feel a presence. The air grows more crowded with those who live there now—a thoroughfare. Lady Franklin, Lady Sarashina: so many hurrying by.

At random, I pick up a magazine—*Audubon*, November-December 1992—and read an article on how the settlers on the Great Plains kept canaries as the only songbirds, the only color, the only delicate beauty possible to them in a lonely world of wind and grass. The author, Roger Welsch, tells the story of a woman who, after hearing him speak on the subject, broke into tears. She finally understood: Among her grandmother's very few possessions she had found a dead canary carefully kept in a small wooden box. She had never known why her grandmother, a Nebraska settler, had so valued it. Now she did: "This gentle creature was perhaps what kept her from walking eastward in the shoulder-high grass until she died, or hanging herself from the well winch—there being nothing like a tree or bridge for a conventional suicide."

Far from the desolate plains or the Arctic seas, Emily Dickinson knew:

> *"Hope" is the thing with feathers—*
> *That perches in the soul—*
> *And sings the tune without the words—*
> *And never stops—at all—*
>
> . . . .
>
> *I've heard it in the chillest land—*
> *And on the strangest Sea—*
> *Yet never, in Extremity,*
> *It asked a crumb—of Me.*

Here is De Long's tomtit searching for the *New York Herald* and his Ross's gulls bringing messages of beauty, his snow bunting, and his final seagull that became soup, that fed them and led them on, a wild communion, into the wild.

Here is Pandora of *Starstuff;* Nigeraurak, the black cat of the *Karluk;* and Vic, the cat of the second Wrangel Island expedition. Here is connection with the world of song and warmth and domestic order, the world beyond silence and water and unforgiving ice. It is the place called home, the place we search the world for, the place we need no map for, and now I must leave: Alexander on a black, red, and white blanket on my broken chair, a blanket given to me as a retirement present by my friend Richard Bunker. Alexander sitting upright on the warm printer, surprised every time the noises happen and paper pushes out over the burnished brown fur of his paws. Alexander, who goes out with me to capture poems and wrestle them down.

NOVEMBER 12

✳ *Shortly after nine this morning the Juneau airport closes down. A military plane on final approach has gone off radar.* The Alaska Army National Guard C-12F with eight on board was last heard from about 9 A.M., reporting its location as Barlow Cove, on the north end of Admiralty Island. It was making an instrument-assisted approach. The airport tower maintained contact with the plane for another ten minutes before there was silence.

Winds up to forty miles per hour, low clouds, rain, and snow were impeding the search.

The plane had left Elmendorf Air Force Base in Anchorage at 7:12 A.M.

In a meeting, I look out the windows. Rain mixed with snow is hurled against the mountains. It is not a day to be flying.

I try to think of other things, concentrate on what is happening around me, but all day my stomach tightens. Where is it? Where are they? Can they be found—in time? Already this week seven have died in three crashes around the state.

Late in the afternoon, the news is broadcast: The wreckage of the twin-engine Beechcraft Super King C-12F has been found by a Coast Guard helicopter, at the 2,600-foot level of the Chilkat mountain range, about twenty-four miles west of Juneau. Eight people were on board, including Brigadier General Thomas Carroll, forty-four, commander of the Alaska Army National Guard. There are no survivors, and no attempt will be made to retrieve the bodies until first light tomorrow. A military investigation team is on its way from Alabama.

It will be a long night for those waiting.

The site is less than two miles from the place where the Alaska Airlines flight crashed in 1971, claiming 111 lives, and close to the spot where the medical evacuation Learjet crashed in 1985, taking four more: all near the only named feature in that part of the Chilkat Peninsula, Teardrop Lake. Apparently, once more the flight crew thought they had cleared the wall of the Chilkats. They had calculated their position to be ten miles east of where they actually were. Here, in town, the weather has cleared. But on the Chilkats, separating us from Lituya Bay and the raging coast, it will keep snowing. The perfect, unique, six-sided crystals will fall in order, covering the bodies as if to protect them. With daylight, investigators and rescuers will assemble in number. If conditions permit, they will fly to the site, where they will examine and prod each inch of the scene, collect every bit of debris, read each mark, the fall of each broken piece. Perhaps they will not be able to.

The night before we left, I was up all night, running up and down the stairs from basement to attic, packing things away, paying bills, filing papers, writing a long letter to the friends who were to move into our house. Over and over I talked to the cat and the dog, telling them I was not abandoning them. There was still much to do. But before the cold dawn came, it was time to leave.

Sometimes a plane, once found, is in too precarious and unstable a position to be approached or is too deeply buried. But for now, the bodies are gently covered with crystals of silence and peace. There is no hope, there is no searching. The compass has ceased to spin. There is only the falling of the snow, the stillness in the sanctuary of true north.

Bibliography

Alaska Geographic. "Alaska's Glaciers," vol. 9, no. 1, 1982.

————. "Where Mountains Meet the Sea: Alaska's Gulf Coast," vol. 13, no. 1, 1986.

————. "Denali," vol. 15, no. 3, 1988.

ALLEN, ARTHUR JAMES. *A Whaler and Trader in the Arctic, 1895–1944: My Life with the Bowhead.* Anchorage: Alaska Northwest, 1978.

ALLEN, EDWARD WEBER. *The Vanishing Frenchman: The Mysterious Disappearance of La Pérouse.* Rutland, Vt.: Charles E. Tuttle, 1959.

ALLEN, EVERETT S. *Children of the Light: The Rise and Fall of New Bedford Whaling and the Death of the Arctic Fleet.* Boston: Little, Brown, 1973.

BANCROFT, HUBERT H. *History of Alaska, 1730–1885.* New York: Antiquarian, 1959.

BARTLETT, CAPTAIN ROBERT A. *The Last Voyage of the* Karluk. Boston: Small, Maynard, 1916.

——. *The Log of Bob Bartlett: The True Story of Forty Years of Seafaring and Exploration.* New York: G. P. Putnam's Sons, 1928.

BENTLEY, W. A., AND W. J. HUMPHREYS. *Snow Crystals.* New York: Dover, 1962.

BERRY, ERICK. *Mr. Arctic: An Account of Vilhjalmur Stefansson.* New York: David McKay, 1966.

BERTON, PIERRE. *The Arctic Grail: The Quest for the North West Passage and the North Pole, 1818–1909.* New York: Viking, 1988.

BOCSTOCE, JOHN R. *Steam Whaling in the Western Arctic.* New Bedford, Mass.: Old Dartmouth Historical Society, 1977.

BOERI, DAVID. *People of the Ice Whale: Eskimos, White Men, and the Whale.* New York: E. P. Dutton, 1983.

BOHN, DAVE. *Glacier Bay: The Land and the Silence.* San Francisco: Sierra Club, 1967.

CALDWELL, FRANCIS E. *Land of the Ocean Mists.* Edmonds, Wash.: Alaska Northwest, 1986.

COATES, KEN, AND BILL MORRISON. *The Sinking of the* Sophia: *Taking the North Down with Her.* Toronto: Oxford University Press, 1990.

DAUENHAUER, RICHARD AND NORA. *Haa Shuka, Our Ancestors: Tlingit Oral Narratives.* Seattle: University of Washington Press, 1987.

——. *Haa Tuwunaagu Yis, for Healing Our Spirit: Tlingit Oratory.* Seattle: University of Washington Press, 1990.

————. *Haa Kusteeyi, Our Culture: Tlingit Life Stories*. Seattle: University of Washington Press, 1994.

DEARMOND, ROBERT N., ed. *Lady Franklin Visits Sitka, Alaska, 1870: The Journal of Sophia Cracroft, Sir John Franklin's Niece*. Anchorage: Alaska Historical Society, 1981.

DE LA CROIX, ROBERT. *Mysteries of the North Pole*. New York: John Day, 1956.

DE LAGUNA, FREDERICA. *Under Mount St. Elias: The History and Culture of the Yakutat Tlingit* (3 vols.). Washington, D.C.: Smithsonian Institution Press, 1972.

DE LONG, EMMA, ed. *The Voyage of the* Jeannette. Boston: Houghton Mifflin, 1883.

EMMONS, GEORGE THORNTON. *The Tlingit Indians*. Edited and with additions by Frederica de Laguna. Seattle: University of Washington Press, 1991.

FEJES, CLAIRE. *People of the Noatak*. New York: Knopf, 1966.

FIENUP-RIORDAN, ANN. *The Real People and the Children of Thunder: The Yupik Eskimo Encounter with Moravian Missionaries John and Edith Kilbuck*. Norman: University of Oklahoma Press, 1991.

FOOTE, SHELBY. *The Civil War: A Narrative* (3 vols.) New York: Vintage, 1986.

FRANKLIN, SIR JOHN. *Narrative of a Second Expedition to the Shores of the Polar Sea, 1825–26–27*. London: John Murray, 1828.

FROST, O. W. "Steller's Sea Cow." *Alaska Fish & Game*, vol. 18, no. 1, January-February 1986.

GIDDINGS, J. LOUIS. *Ancient Men of the Arctic*. New York: Knopf, 1971.

GREELY, MAJOR-GENERAL A. W. *True Tales of Arctic Heroism in the New World*. New York: Charles Scribner's Sons, 1912.

HARRIS, JOHN. *Without a Trace*. New York: Atheneum, 1981.

HEALY, CAPTAIN M. A. *Report of the Cruise of the Revenue Marine Steamer* Corwin *in the Arctic Ocean in the Year 1884*. Washington, D.C.: Government Printing Office, 1889.

HOEHLING, A. A. *The* Jeannette *Expedition: An Ill-fated Journey to the Arctic*. London: Abelard-Schuman, 1967.

HUNT, WILLIAM R. *Stef: A Biography of Vilhjalmur Stefansson, Canadian Arctic Explorer*. Vancouver: University of British Columbia Press, 1986.

KARI, JAMES, AND JAMES FALL, ed. *Shem Pete's Alaska*. Fairbanks: University of Alaska Press, 1987.

KIZZIA, TOM. *The Wake of the Unseen Object: Among the Cultures of Bush Alaska*. New York: Henry Holt, 1991.

McCLINTOCK, SIR FRANCIS L. *The Voyage of the* Fox *in Arctic Seas*. Boston: Ticknor & Fields, 1860.

McKINLAY, WILLIAM LAIRD. Karluk: *The Great Untold Story of Arctic Exploration*. New York: St. Martin's Press, 1976.

MERTON, THOMAS. *Merton in Alaska*. New York: New Directions Press, 1988.

MIRSKY, JEANNETTE. *To the North! The Story of Arctic Exploration from Earliest Times to the Present*. New York: Viking, 1934.

MOWAT, FARLEY. *People of the Deer*. Toronto: Seal Books, 1984.

————. *The Polar Passion*. Boston: *Atlantic*-Little, Brown, 1967.

O'CLAIR, RITA M., ROBERT H. ARMSTRONG, AND RICHARD CARSTENSEN. *The Nature of Southeast*. Anchorage: Alaska Northwest Books, 1992.

OLEKSA, THE VERY REVEREND MICHAEL. "The Death of Hieromonk Juvenaly," in *Russia in North America: Proceedings of the Second International Conference on Russian America—Sitka, Alaska, 1987.* Kingston, Ontario, 1990.

PRICE, A. GRENFELL, ed. *The Explorations of Captain James Cook in the Pacific as Told by Selections of His Own Journals, 1768–1779.* New York: Dover, 1971.

PTOLEMY, CLAUDIUS. *The Geography.* New York: Dover, 1991.

RANSOM, LIEUTENANT COMMANDER M. A., WITH ELOISE KATHERINE EN-GLE. *Sea of the Bear: Journal of a Voyage to Alaska and the Arctic, 1921.* Annapolis: United States Naval Institute, 1964.

RASMUSSEN, KNUD: *Across Arctic America: Narrative of the Fifth Thule Expedition.* New York: Greenwood Press, 1927.

SCHLEY, W. S., AND J. R. SOLEY. *The Rescue of Greely.* New York: Charles Scribner's Sons, 1885.

SHALAMOV, VARLAM. *Graphite.* New York: W. W. Norton, 1981.

———. *Kolyma Tales.* New York: W. W. Norton, 1980.

SHALKOP, ANTOINETTE, ed. *Exploration in Alaska: Captain Cook Commemorative Lectures, June-November, 1978.* Anchorage: Cook Inlet Historical Society, 1980.

SHERWONIT, BILL. *To the Top of Denali.* Anchorage: Alaska Northwest Books, 1990.

STEFANSSON, EVELYN. *Within the Circle: Portrait of the Arctic.* New York: Charles Scribner's Sons, 1945.

STEFANSSON, VILHJALMUR. *The Adventure of Wrangel Island.* New York: MacMillan, 1925.

————. *Discovery: The Autobiography of Vilhjalmur Stefansson*. New York: McGraw-Hill, 1964.

————. *The Friendly Arctic: The Story of Five Years in Polar Regions*. New York: MacMillan, 1943.

STELLER, GEORG WILHELM. *Journal of a Voyage with Bering, 1741–1742*. Edited and with an introduction by O. W. Frost; translated by Margritt A. Engel and O. W. Frost. Stanford: Stanford University Press, 1988.

STOMMEL, HENRY. *Lost Islands: The Story of Islands That Have Vanished from Nautical Charts*. Vancouver: University of British Columbia Press, 1984.

STUCK, HUDSON. *The Ascent of Denali: First Complete Ascent of Mt. McKinley, Highest Peak in North America, Containing the Original Diary of Walter Harper, First Man to Achieve Denali's True Summit*. Seattle: The Mountaineers, 1977.

THORNTON, HARRISON R. *Among the Eskimos of Wales, Alaska*. Baltimore: Johns Hopkins University Press, 1931.

TUTTLE, CAPTAIN FRANCIS. *Report of the Cruise of the U.S. Revenue Cutter* Bear *and the Overland Expedition for the Relief of the Whalers in the Arctic Ocean, November 27, 1897–September 13, 1898*. Washington, D.C.: Government Printing Office, 1899.

VANSTONE, JAMES W. "Alaska Natives and the White Man's Religion: A Cultural Interface in Historical Perspective," in *Exploration in Alaska*, ed. Antoinette Shalkop. Anchorage: Cook Inlet Historical Society, 1980.

————. *Point Hope: An Eskimo Village in Transition*. Seattle: University of Washington Press, 1962.

WEBB, ROBERT LLOYD. *On the Northwest: Commercial Whaling in the Pacific Northwest, 1790–1967.* Vancouver: University of British Columbia Press, 1988.

WILLIAMS, TERRY TEMPEST, AND TED MAJOR. *The Secret Language of Snow.* Santa Fe: Sierra Club/Pantheon, 1984.

WOODMAN, DAVID C. *Unravelling the Franklin Mystery: Inuit Testimony.* Montreal: McGill-Queen's University Press, 1991.

Acknowledgments

With thanks to Robert DeArmond, historian of southeast Alaska, and to the staff of the Alaska State Library: passing on the light.